TREASURE
❦ *for* ❧
THE SOUL

―――❄❄❄―――

A THREE-MONTH DAILY DEVOTION
OF GOD'S PURSUING LOVE

―――❄❄❄―――

RAY BENTLEY

TREASURE *for* THE SOUL
A THREE-MONTH DAILY DEVOTION OF GOD'S PURSUING LOVE

by Ray Bentley

Published by

▲▲ MARANATHA PRESS

© 2017 Ray Bentley. All rights reserved.

Printed in the United States of America
ISBN: 978-1-60039-357-0

For information, write to:

MARANATHA PRESS
10752 Coastwood Road, San Diego, CA. 92127.

Cover and Interior Layout: Brett Burner, Lamp Post

Introduction

"I am my beloved's and my beloved is mine."
Song of Solomon 6:3

I would like to invite you to join me this year on a journey of discovery.

One of the great passions of my life and ministry is to understand and communicate the love of God. As I read and study the many Bible verses that describe God's love, I long to live it and believe it whole-heartedly. I also want those I teach to know our true identity as God's children. To believe and *know* that we are God's *beloved*. To experience His presence in our daily lives, as we uncover the great treasures of truth and life He has for us.

Everything about the Gospel proclaims love, and everything about God's actions demonstrates the ultimate romance of our souls by the One desperately seeking to capture our hearts and bless our lives.

There's no greater way to start the New Year than to open ourselves to the presence and love of God. As we discover His treasure house of blessings, we can transcend the trials of life (not avoid them) and have confidence in the bigger picture, where God has a plan and a purpose, founded in His love for you, personally.

Some years ago I endured a crisis of faith. Everything in my life was challenged. Everything I held dear was threatened. I had nothing to cling to but God's love. And you know what? His love held me. It kept me. The Holy Spirit protected me, taught me, and comforted me—for that is what the Holy Spirit does: comfort, and communicate, above all, the personal, passionate love of God.

Can God's love help you survive a broken heart? Can that love help you rise above personal, financial, and health problems? Can the love of God give you the strength to endure and survive? Can His love give you the ability to cling to Him? Can His Spirit give you the insight to understand some of the mysteries of life? Can we really live in His presence?

I believe the answer to all those questions is yes. God truly does romance our souls, as He gifts us with treasures of knowledge, wisdom, love, and peace to bless our lives. That is what I want to explore in a myriad of ways during this next year.

I feel constrained, compelled, to get this message across. God's love is a great love, full of depths, heights, valleys, and mountains that most of us have barely begun to explore. It is a love that corrects, convicts, comforts, teaches, and saves.

It is a love that will transform and save our lives.

"For I am persuaded that neither death nor life,
nor angels nor principalities nor powers,
nor things present nor things to come,
nor height nor depth, nor any other created thing,
shall be able to separate us from the love of God
which is in Christ Jesus our Lord."

ROMANS 8:38-39

TREASURE
❧ *for* ❧
THE SOUL

January

January 1

You Can Be Confident

"Being confident of this very thing,
that He who has begun a
good work in you will complete it
until the day of Jesus Christ."
PHILIPPIANS 1:6

This has to be one of the most reassuring verses in the Bible. You can be *confident* that God is able to continue the work He has started in your life. As we begin a new year and embark on our resolutions and self-improvement programs, remember, the ultimate "make over" is in the hands of the God who loves you.

No matter how discouraged you feel about yourself or your circumstances, *know* with confidence that God is working. As Pastor Chuck Smith said, "The work of the Spirit of God will continue in you. It is based on the faithfulness of God. He hasn't taken you this far to dump you now!"

I know that we don't always experience that confidence. I worry sometimes that I might mess things up so badly that failure is the only outcome. But you know what? Sometimes failure *is* the only outcome. Sometimes we just can't make happen what we want to happen. We can't always change ourselves. We can't be who we want to be or live up to others' expectations. And, we can't change other people.

It's maddening—and sometimes depressing. Even the apostle Paul cried out one day in sheer frustration and spiritual agony: *"O wretched man that I am! Who will deliver me from this body of death?"* (Romans 7:24).

Who? Hebrews 12:2 reminds us who: "Looking unto Jesus, the author and finisher of our faith." Paul knew who would never leave him nor forsake him. Who would continue to work in his life.

God, through Jesus Christ, will continue to work out the plan for our lives that He ordained from the foundations of the world. He knows who we are. He knows our weakness and vulnerabilities. He doesn't want us to ignore those parts of our lives or fear them. He knows what it will take for us to stay close to Him. He will allow events and circumstances that will help us

know without a doubt, that nothing will ever separate us from His love. We can always live in God's presence.
What a relief!

"We know that to those who love God,
who are called according to His plan,
everything that happens fits into a pattern for good"
Romans 8:28

J.B. Phillips, *THE NEW TESTAMENT IN MODERN ENGLISH*

January 2

We All Need Friends

"Grace to you and peace
from God our Father
and the Lord Jesus Christ.
I thank my God upon
every remembrance of you."
PHILIPPIANS 1:2-3

There is something terribly wrong in the church today. People are devoted to God, committed to His work, willing to burn themselves out in service of the Kingdom. But we are somehow unconnected to the emotions and heart needs of our own lives, and of those around us.

Paul was in prison when he wrote the passage above. He knew how his imprisonment would affect his flock. He wrestled with the impact it was having on him. We've all heard expressions like *"Grace to you and peace from God"* in some form, to the point where they become meaningless, like saying hello.

But to Paul these words weren't casual clichéd greetings. He knew how important it was for his readers to trust in God's grace, to experience His peace. He wasn't writing just as an apostle to the church; he was writing friend to friend; very warm, very personal. He wanted to encourage his readers. Yes, he was imprisoned, yes, his life was threatened, but we can count on God's grace and peace. And he wasn't afraid to admit that he *needed* to count on them, because his life was hard and scary.

He was thankful for his friends. Every time he thought of them, every moment he sat there in prison, alone, he knew someone cared, someone was praying. **He stopped to thank God every time he remembered them.** Paul was connected to his brothers and sisters in Christ, emotionally and spiritually, even if he was separated physically.

We need to be there for each other. We are a body, and we can bless each other . . . or we can ignore each other. Part of the secret of Paul's strength and joy was the intimate, close fellowship he had with other believers.

Intimate fellowship is what God desires for us and is one of the most powerful ways He demonstrates His love toward us. Stop to thank God for your friends and reach out to someone who needs a friend!

"To live in prayer together is to walk in love together."

MARGARET MOORE JACOBS

January 3

God's Family

"For God is my witness, how greatly I long for
you all with the affection of Jesus Christ."
PHILIPPIANS 1:8

The emotion in Paul's declaration is strong. He's not just telling friends he misses them. He's not just wondering how things are going at the office or in the neighborhood. The words used here describe deep, inner affections. He is separated from people he deeply loves and is not afraid to say so.

Have you ever gone on vacation and just relished being *away* for those first few days? New places and new people are interesting and distracting, for the moment. But eventually our thoughts and yearnings turn toward home, our family, and to friends of long standing whose lives are interwoven with ours.

Not everyone is part of a close family, with parents, cousins, brothers, and sisters. Some families are painful and difficult and maybe you don't miss being away from them. But a church family, fellow believers who love Jesus—while not perfect, and also difficult at times—can fill an important need in our lives. In fact, the family of believers is *meant* to fill a need.

"The factor that most significantly determines my new identity as a Christian is not the blood of my biological family, but the blood of Jesus. We are given a new name (Christian), a new inheritance (freedom, glory, hope, resources a hundredfold), and new power (the Holy Spirit) . . . and able to enjoy the absolute security and stability, freedom, intimacy, and confidence in prayer of children in God's family," Pastor Peter Scazzero writes.

When I think of the apostle Paul writing, in prison, about his Christian brothers and sisters, I can picture him, chained to a soldier, a wave of nostalgia sweeping over him as he longs for the warmth and welcome of his friend Lydia's home, for the hearty embrace of the jailer who had become his brother in Christ, and for the sweet hugs of the jailer's children. Little is mentioned in Scripture of Paul's biological family.

If you don't have this kind of relationship with your brothers and sisters in Christ, then I encourage you to nurture bonds of fellowship. **Get into small group studies, reach out to others, bear one another's burdens.** Pray for each other, and soon you will find yourself loving each other, with a common bond of Jesus and His inexhaustible love.

"And this is His commandment: that we should believe
on the name of His Son Jesus Christ and love one another."

1 JOHN 3:23

January 4

Living on the Vine

"I am the true vine, and My Father is the vinedresser.
Every branch in Me that does not bear fruit He takes away;
and every branch that bears fruit He prunes,
that it may bear more fruit . . . Abide in Me and I in you.
As the branch cannot bear fruit of itself,
unless it abides in the vine,
neither can you, unless you abide in Me."
JOHN 15:1-4

We're almost a week into the New Year, and have had time to reflect upon what God wants for us this year. As I prayed for the new year, waiting on the Lord, He whispered in my ear, *presence. My presence.* He wants us to live in His presence! To draw closer to Him, in a deep, personal relationship, experiencing His presence.

The presence of God can be a bit scary, can't it? It reminds me of the story of Aslan in the *Chronicles of Narnia* by C.S. Lewis. Aslan the lion is an allegorical figure representing Christ. One of the main characters, Lucy, asks Mrs. Beaver about Aslan: "Then he isn't safe?"

"Safe?" said Mrs. Beaver. "Who said anything about safe? 'Course he isn't safe. But he's good. He's the King, I tell you."

No, God is not always "safe." He doesn't allow us to remain as we are. He challenges us to grow and stretch and deal with problems head on. He takes us places we're not sure we want to go. But, as Mrs. Beaver said, He is good! We can trust Him. We can abandon our fears and go for intimacy with our heavenly Father, because we can trust in His goodness.

I know the world doesn't seem very safe right now. All of us feel the uncertainty of change, terrorism, dangerous world issues—and personal struggles as well. Many of our lives are in crisis.

The answer to that, and to living in the presence of God, begins with the verse above, in John 15. Notice, the only responsibility of the branch (us) is to abide in Christ. All the rest—the pruning, the cleansing, the nurturing, strengthening—all of it is the vinedresser's responsibility. And that is exactly what He is doing.

Pruning our hearts through circumstances, hardships, and changes, so that we will draw closer to His heart.

To all who are weary, frightened or unsure of the future, Jesus says, "Let not your hearts be troubled," and "Follow Me."

Jesus is God's love manifested in human form. He is the Father's way of saying, "I love you, I want to bless you, draw you closer to Me, and give you a life of joy, peace, and love."

May we all cling to the Vine in this new year!

January 5

Fatness!

"Though by this time you ought to be teachers,
you need someone to teach you the
elementary truths of God's word all over again.
You need milk, not solid food!
Anyone who lives on milk, being still an infant,
is not acquainted with the teaching about righteousness.
But solid food is for the mature,
who by constant use have trained themselves
to distinguish good from evil."
HEBREWS 5:13-14 NIV

God likes food. One of His greatest gifts to us is the enjoyment of nourishment, physically and spiritually. Food and drink metaphors run throughout the Bible, from the moment Eve ate the apple. *Fruit of the Spirit . . . the land of milk and honey . . . Jesus as the Bread* *of life . . . living water . . . new wine . . . the milk and strong meat of the Word*, are a few.

In the verse above, the writer distinguishes between "milk" and "meat," which is solid food. Milk is predigested food for babies. *You could have been teachers by now!* the writer says. But you aren't ready. You're still living on milk and need someone to teach you meat.

The milk of the Word is defined here as "elementary truths of God's Word." Milk teaches us basic facts of our faith: the life of Jesus. His birth, death, burial, resurrection, and ascension. We never outgrow our need for "milk."

But to mature as a believer, and grow into someone who is discerning, insightful, who understands good and evil, and can experience the fullness of God's blessings, you need to move on to a daily diet of solid spiritual food. You need to grasp the deeper, living, levels of understanding that God Word delivers, and then incorporate those truths into daily life.

Milk is hearing about the life of Jesus. Meat is *living* the life of Jesus.

Our spiritual "muscle" can only be developed by exercising God's Word in our lives.

Make the study of God's Word your steady diet this year. Go beyond the basics and dig in. Take in God's

Word, digest it, let it nourish your soul and spirit, and enjoy it for the rich, abundant, and altogether satisfying feast that it is!

> *"Let your soul delight itself in fatness."*
> ISAIAH 55:2

January 6

How I Long to Live

"But what does it matter?
The important thing is that in every way,
whether from false motives or true,
Christ is preached. And because of this I rejoice.
Yes, and I will continue to rejoice."
PHILIPPIANS 1:18

The apostle Paul was in prison. In prison! **Did God make a mistake allowing this?** How could He allow this warrior of the cross to be shut up like this? Just when he was doing so much good.

Have you ever felt like that? Just when things were going so well—wham! It all came to a screeching halt over some unfortunate circumstance.

And of course, when that happens, people start to talk. And to judge. *Well,* they say, *God must be dealing in his life . . . she must be doing something terribly wrong . . . makes you wonder what's really going on . . .*

Satan is called "the accuser of the brethren" for a reason (Revelation 12:10). He loves to stir up trouble among believers with innuendo, implied wrongdoing, gossip, and doubt about one another's faith and character. He loves to cause fellow believers to lay guilt trips on each other.

Paul had his share of critics who loved to accuse him of all sorts of wrongdoing and ill motives. Some were jealous. Others just plain didn't like him. Some grieved over his imprisonment. Others were just as glad he was out of the way for a while. But Paul had learned a secret about rising above such circumstances. He didn't run from his despair or hardship. He didn't live in denial. He lived in absolute faith that God knows what He's doing.

> *"And we know that all things work together
> for good to those who love God,
> to those who are the called
> according to His purpose."*
> ROMANS 8:28

Paul knew his purpose: to preach the Gospel. So no matter how it happened, in prison or out, through good motives or impure ones—he was able to rejoice because ultimately God was fulfilling His purposes in Paul's life.

That's how I long to live—rejoicing, in the midst of tears, laughter, pain, or joy—knowing that in it all, God's love never fails.

January 7

A Purpose for Being Alive!

"I can hardly wait to continue on my course.
I don't expect to be embarrassed in the least.
On the contrary, everything happening to me
in this jail only serves to make
Christ more accurately known,
regardless of whether I live or die.
They didn't shut me up; they gave me a pulpit!"
PHILIPPIANS 1:20 MSG

The author of those words, the apostle Paul, knew his *purpose* **for being alive,** for existing on this earth. He didn't necessarily know what he was going to be *doing* all the time, but he knew why God created him. And because of that, he was excited about life. Listen to him: "I can hardly wait to continue on my course." Oh that we would all wake up every day feeling like that!

Paul was free—even in prison. He possessed a kind of freedom I wish we all could know. He had learned to be vulnerable, open, his weaknesses exposed, his faults on display, his failures open to public conjecture. But he knew why he was alive.

The logo for a missionary organization displays an ox on one side, an altar on the other, and the words, "Ready for Either." Ready to work, ready to worship. Ready for life, ready for death. That is how Paul lived. He could be set free. Or he could be executed. The door could swing either way, and he was ready.

Paul had one goal in life: to bring Jesus closer to people. To allow others to see Jesus through his life, to let people see His glory and grace. It is hard to see *God's* glory and grace in people who seem perfect, intimidating, and super successful. So Paul had to live his life in prison, and in public, letting the world see how Jesus overcame his failures, strengthened his weaknesses, and worked through him in spite of his shortcomings.

Jesus had one goal during His life on earth: to show humanity the Father. He accomplished that through public ministry, or by just hanging out with people. His life was filled with joy when He healed and taught, or with sorrow as He wept for those who hurt. He was admired and worshiped. He was hated, He was rejected . . . and He was crucified. All so that we would come to know the Father.

"The Word became flesh and made His dwelling among us," His friend John wrote. *"We have seen His glory, the glory of the One and Only, who came from the Father, full of grace and truth"* (John 1:14 NIV).

> "Man, made in the image of God, has a purpose—to be in relationship to God, who is there. Man forgets his purpose and thus he forgets who he is and what life means."
>
> Francis Schaeffer

January 8

To Live Is . . .

"For me to live is Christ . . . "
PHILIPPIANS 1:21

"For me to live is . . . "

If someone asked you to finish that sentence without much time to think, what would you say?

For me to live is . . . sports? Shopping? Music? Family? Work? The person I'm in love with? Fill in the blank.

But if I can say in all sincerity "to live is Christ," then I can follow that bold statement with what comes next: "to die is gain."

Paul—apostle, missionary, former Pharisee, and persecutor of the church—lost a lot before he was able to make such a bold statement. I don't know if I can say that I always feel like "to die is gain." I love my life and want to hang onto it and to the people I love.

Paul's life had been filled with prestige, education, and respect—until he experienced a radical conversion. That's when his life began to unravel. He became mistrusted, persecuted, reviled, even hated. He developed a physical infirmity, which no amount of prayer healed. "Three times I pleaded with the Lord to take it away from me," Paul wrote. "But He said to me, 'My grace is sufficient for you, for my power is made perfect in weakness'" (2 Corinthians 12:8-10).

Becoming a Christian made Paul capable of recognizing his weaknesses. He became more honest, vulnerable, and broken—real. He shared freely how difficult, fractured, and broken he was. He had no need to protect his image, or misrepresent who he was.

He set an example for us of how to live at home, in the workplace, in the world. He simply let the Lord work through him as he labored to strengthen and build up people, demonstrating the love of God.

In all this, he was content, happy, and so committed that he could exclaim, "For me to live is Christ!"

He had discovered what it means to be truly alive.

"Fear not that your life shall come to an end, but rather that it shall never have a beginning."

JOHN HENRY NEWMAN

January 9

Interesting but Not Interested

"Fulfill my joy . . .
Let nothing be done through
selfish ambition or conceit,
but in lowliness of mind let each
esteem others better than himself.
Let each of you look out not only
for his own interests,
but also for the interests of others."
PHILIPPIANS 2:2-4

Connecting with people fills us with joy. The best therapy for our angst and dissatisfaction is giving, receiving, and working out things together. "I hope to visit you and talk to you face to face," wrote the apostle John, "so that our joy might be complete" (2 John 12).

But connecting with people is more than hanging out and interacting. Author Mike Mason wrote of an incident when he was on a plane, and being in a good mood, struck up a conversation with a young man. The time passed quickly, and they covered a lot of conversational territory. Then he says, "It dawned on me that as much as I enjoyed our conversation, it was not the young man I had enjoyed so much as my own charm and conviviality. I'd been absorbed in being interesting without being truly interested."[1]

I hate it when that happens.

Haven't we all been guilty of being "interesting without being truly interested?" That reduces people to mere reflections of us, our egos, and our interests— rather than us seeing other people as reflections of God and His interests.

"In lowliness of mind let each esteem others better than himself," the apostle wrote (above).

Wow. Do we really look at others with admiration and esteem, thinking, "You know, in spite of her problems and trials, she is better than me. She handles her lot in life better than I could."

But what joy we will find—indeed we are promised—if we can take these Scriptures to heart and look at other people with a genuine desire to care for their cares, to see them as God sees them—and as the reason we are still here on this earth.

> "There is nothing more truly artistic than to love people."
>
> —VINCENT VAN GOGH[2]

1. Mason, Mike, *Practicing the Presence of People* (Waterbrook Press, Colorado Springs, 1999).
2. Vincent Van Gogh, Irving Stone, Jean Stone, *Dear Theo: The Autobiography of Vincent Van Gogh* (Plume, 1995) p. 339.

January 10

Can You Restore God's Image?

"Sitting down, Jesus called the Twelve and said,
'If anyone wants to be first,
he must be the very last,
and the servant of all.'"
MARK 9:33-35 NIV

Last, and the servant of all. Hard words to live.

Mother Teresa taught us about servanthood. She represents a host of believers scattered throughout history and the world, who will never be famous, will seldom receive acknowledgment for their service, but who are great people. Period.

How do they do it? What motivates their hearts? How can someone like Mother Teresa give up so much, spend so much of her life amongst the poorest, dirtiest, most forgotten segments of humanity?

"She went to gutters and garbage heaps, to places where humanity itself had been thrown away and left to rot, and she set to work patiently and tenderly restoring to people the dignity of being human . . . Mother Teresa's days began in prayer, and after meeting God in prayer she went out into the streets of Calcutta to meet Him in the form of people . . . her primary goal was not to better the lot of the poor, not to alleviate the suffering of the sick, not even to save lives. Rather, her goal was to recover the image of God in people."[1]

Mother Teresa accomplished her mission, one person at a time. Looking into the dirty, smudged faces of the sad, the poor, and the diseased (which is all of us in some form), she gently wiped away the dirt, cupping a small face in her hands, and smiling into those eyes, she communicated love and acceptance. And then, I just know, she saw the reflection of God; she restored the image of God in a person who the rest of the world would have thrown away.

Can we do any less with the people around us? People whose lives are marred and smudged with burdens that weigh them down and create anxiety, unrest, and unhappiness. Can we love and serve one such person back into God's image? Can we walk out of our doors every morning and expect to witness God's glory in the lives of our family, friends, and co-workers? Can we throw down our egos, our lives, our self-importance, and be *the servant of all?*

1. Mason, Mike, *Practicing the Presence of People* (Waterbrook Press, Colorado Springs, 1999

January 11

Pour Love

"Your attitude should be the same as that of Christ Jesus:
Who, being in very nature God,
did not consider equality with God
something to be grasped,
but made Himself nothing,
taking the very nature of a servant,
being made in human likeness."
PHILIPPIANS 2:5-7 NIV

A guy comes into the church, says he wants to serve God and is available—what can he do? Once when this happened at our church, the most pressing need at the moment was to get the front sidewalks swept before the evening service—they were a mess. The guy reluctantly took a broom, did a halfhearted job, thanked us for the "opportunity" and left.

There was no intention to insult him, but he later admitted that his attitude was pretty unservant-like. "I was fuming," he said. "I tell you guys I want to serve the Lord and someone hands me a broom. I'm thinking, *I HIRE people to sweep my sidewalks . . . don't they know who I am and how much I have contributed to the church?* I just didn't get it—until later when I began to understand the nature of Jesus."

Picture Jesus as He lived, touching the lepers, the lame, the unlovely, healing the sick and befriending the poor. Jesus dined with sinners, ministered to prostitutes, and was surrounded by clamoring throngs of people who wanted to touch the hem of His garment. Jesus walked amongst humanity, not afraid to "get dirty" or to pour love into their lives. God loves us, woos us, and pursues us. This was part of His great pursuit—denying Himself the power of the Godhead, the glory of heaven, and becoming one of us. He denied Himself to love us, so that we can deny ourselves to love Him back, and in turn, love others.

"We can do little things for God: I turn the cake that is frying on the pan, for love of Him; and that done, if there is nothing else to call me, I prostrate myself in worship before Him who has given me grace to work; afterward I rise happier than a king."

BROTHER LAWRENCE[1]

1. Quoted in: *Living Quotations for Christians*, edited by Sherwood Eliot Wirt and Kersten Beckstrom, copyright 1974, Harper and Row Publishers, Inc.,New York, NY., p. 148, ref. 1985.

January 12

Step Down

"And being found in appearance as a man,
He humbled Himself and became obedient
to the point of death, even the death of the cross."
PHILIPPIANS 2:8

Jesus manifested His greatness by taking steps down.
While the rest of the world is intent on climbing up—
up the corporate ladder, up to a better neighborhood,
up to higher education, higher office—Jesus stepped
down, for us.

He was God, equal with God, and He deliberately
emptied Himself and came to earth in the form of a
humble servant. Jesus stepped down from glory and
equality with almighty God, to the cruel Roman cross,
where He hung for our sins before an angry, jeering
mob, despised and rejected by mankind.

That's a big step down, from the highest height to the lowest, most humiliating death known to the world at that time, death upon the cross.

Stepping down is hard. To give up something you've worked hard to attain or even to let go of a position that you know isn't right for you. Or to volunteer for a job that seems beneath your level of education or competence. But if you feel that tug of the Holy Spirit calling you to let it go, to humble yourself, let go of the ego or the need to be in charge, and step down to serve others, remember what Jesus did for us. And through obedience, you will also know great joy.

> "There is, therefore, something in humility which, strangely enough, exalts the heart."
>
> St. Augustine [1]

---

1. Augustine, *City of God*, book XIV, ch. 13.

January 13

And He Will Lift You Up

"Humble yourselves in the sight of the Lord,
and He will lift you up."
JAMES 4:10

The Christian life is a paradox. We die to ourselves to live. We give to receive. The first shall be last. We can only be lifted up if we willingly step down. And we can't do any of the first steps with the sole intention and motive of receiving the second part of the paradox. We are called to abandon ourselves to faith—but not to be stupid just for the sake of testing God and getting what we want.

"For whoever desires to save his life will lose it, but whoever loses his life for My sake will find it," Jesus said, explaining how this works (Matthew 16:25).

Jesus stepped down from Glory, and was ultimately lifted up. His resurrection was prophesied and promised. *"Because you will not abandon me to the grave, nor will you let your Holy One see decay"* (Psalm 16:10).

Jesus went from Glory to Glory—but in between, was the Cross.

The Lord will not abandon us to a grave of despair or failure, nor will He allow our lives to be decayed by sin. He died for us, that we might live in victory, in the abundant life He longs for us to live. First comes brokenness, vulnerability, humility—then the tender mercy of God as He lifts us up to live in the comfort of His grace and love.

January 14

Fasting and Praying[1]

"Prayer is nothing else than a sense of God's presence."

BROTHER LAWRENCE.

"Do you have a hunger for God? If we don't feel strong desires for the manifestation of the glory of God, it is not because we have drunk deeply and are satisfied. It is because we have nibbled so long at the table of the world. Our soul is stuffed with small things, and there is no room for the great. If we are full of what the world offers, then perhaps a fast might express, or even increase, our soul's appetite for God."

JOHN PIPER

At some point near the first of the year, I plan, with my church, to set aside 40 days for prayer and fasting.

We start our New Year by asking God to manifest His presence in our lives, allowing us to "drink deeply" and sense God's presence as the quotes above say.

During the 40 days, I encourage those participating to go to "higher ground." **Find a local mountain, a view from the top of a building, or the hill behind your house. Go to higher ground and pray, asking God to manifest His presence over all that you see.**

Praying and fasting is a biblical practice that gives us the opportunity to focus on the Lord and to find extra time and energy to pray and hear God's voice and experience His presence.

Numerous examples of fasting in the Bible include:

- Moses Fasted Before Receiving the
  Commandments – *Deuteronomy 9:9-18*

- David Mourning His Child's Illness
  – *2 Samuel 12:1-23*

- Elijah Fasted While Escaping Jezebel
  – *1 Kings 19:4-8*

- Ezra Fasted While Mourning Over Sin
  – *Ezra 10:6-17*

- Esther Fasted for the Safety of the Jews
  – *Esther 4:15-17*

- Daniel Fasted for an Answer to Prayer
  – *Daniel 10:1-3*

- Jesus Fasted Before Temptation by Satan
  – *Matthew 4:1-2*

- Paul Fasted After His Conversion – *Acts 9:1-9*[2]

I suggest you pray for three things:

- To experience the presence of God.

- Ask God to bring down strongholds and break the idols in your life—anything that would hold back God's outpouring of blessings.

- Revival! May God's blessings down pour and overflow in our lives!

I like what John Piper said above. Our souls are stuffed with "small things and there is no room for the great." I can think of nothing greater than hearing God speak and experiencing His presence in our lives.

A fast will impact other lives. John Wesley said, "Bear up the hands that hang down, by faith and prayer; support the tottering knees. Have you any days of fasting and prayer? Storm the throne of grace and persevere, and mercy will come down."

Pray and ask the Lord to show you how to fast, then prepare for a wonderful 40 days of living in God's presence and experiencing His love.

May this time be a wonderful revelation of God's power and presence!

1. We recognize that fasting is an individual, personal time between you and the Lord. Choose the fast that is best for you. While fasting means abstaining from food for most people, it can also be abstaining from something else to give you deeper time in prayer and fellowship with the Lord. Not everyone can fast from food, but if you give up something in order to focus on the Lord, that can be a meaningful fast. St. Augustine recognized this when he wrote, "If you are not able to keep a fast today, at least partake of food with moderation."

2. Read more: http://www.whatchristianswanttoknow.com/fasting-in-the-bible-10-examples-to-learn-from/#ixzz3xoEU3iJY

January 15

The Key to Blessings

"For the Word of God is living and active.
Sharper than any double-edged sword, it penetrates
even to dividing soul and spirit, joints and marrow;
it judges the thoughts and attitudes of the heart."
HEBREWS 4:12

God is at work in you. You can hinder His work, or receive it and let Him shape your present and future. There is a key to receiving the blessings that go with the process.

Many of us started January of the new year eagerly, with great intentions. Exercise. Eat right. Follow a program to help us grow spiritually. This is the year to get it right.

If you stick with any resolution, make God's Word the priority, with the right motives.

When I was young, I studied the Word zealously, approaching the Bible with a list of questions, determined to find answers. Nothing wrong with that, except that often my motives were skewed by my desire to dazzle others with my vast Bible knowledge. But as I matured, the Word worked in my life. I began to realize the depth, the riches, the power God's Word has in my life. I see something new every time I read even familiar passages and long told stories. Now, I can honestly say, I don't know as much now as I thought I did 20 years ago.

God's Word is living, piercing, and works in our lives in ways we cannot fathom.

A linear philosophy depicts life as a straight line, past to future. Since the past is gone, the future unknowable, the emphasis becomes the present. All that matters is now.

But in the Hebrew culture, in which God's Word was inspired, life is a circle. Recorded histories take meticulous care to recount events, records, and genealogies. The past and its lessons are a window to our future. When you first learn a truth, it is only on one level. Each time we return to that lesson, in life or in history, we gain a new level of understanding and enlightenment. We never fully arrive—we just keep going deeper and higher and gaining new understanding. Studying God's Word is like that.

This year, allow God's Word into your life consistently. It will change you, inspire you, and lead you into greater understanding of your God, of yourself, and of your world.

January 16

Free At Last!

"There is therefore no condemnation for those who are in Christ."
ROMANS 8:1

During this week we honor the memory of Dr. Martin Luther King, Jr., the great civil rights leader who gave us one of the most celebrated lines in modern speech. Quoting an old spiritual, he stood on the steps of the Lincoln Memorial August 28, 1963, and proclaimed to his listeners:

"Free at last! Free at last! Thank God Almighty, we are free at last!"

He referred to the hope and dream of a day when "all of God's children, black men and white men, Jews and gentiles, Protestants and Catholics, will be able to join hands and sing." He was talking about freedom from prejudice and discrimination.

But he also understood spiritual freedom. During his Birmingham civil rights campaign, Dr. King asked participants to pledge to "meditate daily on the teachings and life of Jesus" and to "walk and talk in the manner of love, for God is love" and "pray daily to be used by God in order that all men might be free."[1] He knew the secret to freedom.

Nowhere is spiritual freedom more proclaimed than in Romans 8:1, one of the boldest, most freeing and revolutionary statements found in any sacred writing: "There is therefore no condemnation for those who are in Christ."

Condemnation is a curse. It is a poison on the planet that leads to despair, discouragement and religious fanaticism that cultivates terrorism and racism. Condemnation is a spiritual life gone wrong.

Condemnation is easy to recognize because:

- You feel *guilty* all the time.

- You're *fearful*.

- You live with a profound sense of *rejection*. You might know intellectually that God has accepted you and forgiven you, but you don't feel loved or accepted. This can cause you to reject others through prejudice or fear.

The Christian life is an exchange. We exchange an old life for a new one. Bad habits with new ones. A sentence of death for the gift of eternal life. We replace fear with freedom.

You cannot be free and be controlled by fear. Fear is the worst kind of tyranny and oppression. It hinders life and paralyzes its victims. Fear quenches the Spirit, and deceives us into forgetting our Heavenly Father, who promises, "For I know the thoughts I think toward you . . . thoughts of peace and not evil, to give you a future and a hope" (Jeremiah 29:11).

Romans 8:1 is one of the most liberating statements to ring through eternity. And, for those who have given their lives to Jesus, it is the truth that will set us free and help us to love others without fear and prejudice.

When I contemplate this powerful Scripture, I want to echo the words of Martin Luther King, celebrate, and cry with joy, "Free at last, thank God Almighty, we are free at last!"

1. Charles Colson, *Martin Luther King and Religious Freedom*, http://www1.cbn.com/biblestudy/martin-luther-king-and-religious-freedom

January 17

No One Wants to Be Uriah Heep

*"Therefore, humble yourselves under the mighty hand of God,
that He may exalt you in due time."*
1 PETER 5:6

We talk about being humble a lot in church. We see Jesus' example. We regard some people as humble. But I'm not sure it's that easy to wake up one day and decide to be . . . humble. We may desire to be, but becoming humble is a work that God does in our hearts, through circumstances that remind us of just how human we really are.

Uriah Heep is a villainous character in Charles Dickens' novel, *David Copperfield*. Known for rubbing his hands together and declaring, "I'm so 'umble," Uriah Heep's name became synonymous with a hypocritically humble person. He personified false humility.

None of us intends to be a "Uriah Heep." But what keeps us from being humble? What did Jesus let go of? Everything that would tempt Him with pride. Position. Strength. The invulnerability He possessed as God. He allowed Himself to be broken and vulnerable.

"Leadership in the kingdom of God is from the bottom up, not a grasping, controlling, or lording it over others. It is leading out of failure and pain, questions and struggles—a serving that lets go," writes Peter Scazzero.[1]

Spiritually—and emotionally—healthy people are humble, because they allow themselves to be real, to be broken, vulnerable, and to let go, because Jesus did.

1. Scazzero, Peter, *The Emotionally Healthy Church* (Zondervan, Grand Rapids, Michigan, 2003

January 18

Who Are You?

"Behold what manner of love the Father has bestowed on us."
1 JOHN 3:1

Who are you? Do you wonder why you are here and what your life means?

A young man, college age, nervously fiddles with the edge of the big Bible on his lap. He sits in our church counseling office and says he's confused. About life . . . about his future . . . about God. "I just don't know who I really am," he admits.

A middle-aged man realizes that his life hasn't followed his dreams. He's feeling his age. He's tired of his job. His kids are growing up and growing distant. He questions everything from his marriage to his faith. He looks in the mirror and wonders who that person is and what his life is all about.

A busy woman, with a family, a job, and lists of commitments that keep her running and worn out often stops in her rare quiet moments and wonders, "Is this who I am? Is this what I am meant to be doing?"

The human race suffers from a huge identity crisis! Most of us don't realize who we are, and who we are meant to be.

We are God's creation, made in His image. Thousands of years of sin, corruption, sorrow, and disease may have broken us down into something barely recognizable to anyone who could had known Adam and Eve in their before-the-fall state. But we are still God's creation!

He sent His Son, Jesus, to restore us and to make us alive through His Spirit. He makes us "new creatures" and gives us a new identity. We may carry the outward marks of this world, but our souls and spirits are once again back in the garden with Him.

Through Him we are "renewed in the spirit" of our minds (Ephesians 4:23), we will never thirst (John 4:14), never perish (John 3:16), and we can know and experience the width, length, depth, and height of the love of Christ (Ephesians 3:18-19).

Who are we?

We are children of God (John 1:12) and friends of God (John 15:14). We are servants of the Almighty, and heirs to all that He has to give us (Romans 8:17). God calls His people His "beloved" throughout Scripture.

"I am my beloved's and my beloved is mine!" the *Song of Solomon* proclaims.

Remember who you are. **God's beloved.**

January 19

Honest Sorrow

"Jesus cried out with a loud voice, saying,
'My God, my God, why have you forsaken me?'"
MATTHEW 27:46

Jesus, God's most beloved, knew about glory and power and love. He also knew great sorrow. And He didn't run from it, gloss over it, or pretend that sadness and distress weren't present in His life. He wept over Lazarus, He cried over Jerusalem. And on the cross, He cried the ancient cry of the psalmist as He poured out the words that came from His broken heart. "My God! Why have You forsaken Me?"

I am all for praising God. I believe in the power of praise and worship. But I also know there are times when God knows we need to grieve, and we need to be honest about our sorrow. Jesus on the cross didn't cry out, "Praise God from whom all blessings flow! Victory is mine!" or any such thing. He cried in agony and flung His pain and heartache out to His Father.

Will there be victory? Will there be healing? Yes. God promises it. Here, and in the hereafter. There is a resurrection after the crucifixion. But in the meantime, it is no sin to honestly hurt and grieve. In fact, it is a sin not to.

> *"And God will wipe away every tear from their eyes;*
> *there shall be no more death, nor sorrow,*
> *nor crying. There shall be no more pain,*
> *for the former things have passed away."*
> REVELATION 21:4

January 20

Pressing On

"I press on, that I may lay hold of that for which
Christ Jesus has also laid hold of me.
Brethren, I do not count myself to have apprehended;
but one thing I do, forgetting those things
which are behind and reaching forward
to those things which are ahead,
I press toward the goal for the prize
of the upward call of God in Christ Jesus."
PHILIPPIANS 3:12-14

The apostle Paul was running a race. We just finished watching a spectacular Super Bowl. We know the hard work and perseverance that goes into being an athlete at that level.

But Paul was running a more important race, one that began when he was struck down on the road to

Damascus, surrounded by a heavenly light and the voice of Jesus.

Again, the paradox. He began his race by falling down, overwhelmed by his experience. When he got up, he was blind. Three days later the Lord sent Ananias to pray and lay hands on Paul. Paul's sight was restored, he was filled with the Holy Spirit, baptized into the faith and ready to fulfill God's purpose for his life.

Paul forged ahead. He had a history of pride, of persecuting believers, of being hated and reviled. He did a lot of things wrong! But he repented, and now he had a purpose. Because of Paul's past, many believers didn't trust him. But now he had a chance to make amends, and to demonstrate the sincerity of his faith and love. He couldn't let the past hold him back or bog him down.

My brothers and sisters, I know our lives are filled with past mistakes, sin, pain, regret, and hurtful things done to us or by us. I also know that God forgives and redeems and urges us forward.

He promises, "If we confess our sins, He is faithful and just to forgive us our sins and to cleanse us from all unrighteousness" (1 John 1:9).

"Life can only be understood backward; it must be lived forward."

SØREN KIERKEGAARD[1]

---

1. Quoted in: *Living Quotations for Christians*, edited by Sherwood Eliot Wirt and Kersten Beckstrom, copyright 1974, Harper and Row Publishers, Inc.,New York, NY., p. 144, ref. 1940.

January 21

What Becomes of the Brokenhearted?

*"He heals the brokenhearted
and binds up their wounds."*
PSALM 147:3

The lyrics to that old song are haunting.[1] They speak of broken dreams, disillusion, and confusion. A broken heart is a wound to the soul. Loss, betrayal, misunderstandings, and fear of the unknown can affect you so deeply that you feel a pain in your chest and wonder how you will bear it. Sometimes we grieve for another's sorrow or pain and make it our own.

What becomes of the brokenhearted? Too many cover their hurt with false bravado or phony optimism. They numb their pain with busy work, drugs, drink, entertainment . . . whatever works for a while.

Temporary band-aids for a wound that needs deep cleansing and healing.

When brokenhearted people allow God's Holy Spirit into their hearts, He promises to tend and heal their wounds. Does this happen in a second? Do the pain and the problems disappear at the utterance of a prayer? Not usually.

Notice that the Scripture above promises healing and binding. The binding process is like caring for a physical trauma. Recognizing the wound, understanding the cause, then cleansing and eradicating infection are crucial to the process.

God does the same work in our hearts. No quick band-aids and temporary pain relief. Rather, a deep, life-changing work of the Holy Spirit which drives us closer to God, our Great Physician.

He will take us to the foot of the Cross, where His blood was poured out for the sins that inflict such pain and heartache upon the world. He will expose our wounds, root out the causes and cleanse us from the infection of bitterness and sin. His Comforter, the Holy Spirit, will hold our hands, reminding us, "all things work together for good to those who love God, to those who are the called according to His purpose" (Romans 8:28)!

And then, blessed relief! His promises are true. And from the depths of our tender and healing heart, He can now begin to manifest the attributes of His Spirit: love, joy, peace, patience and all the gifts God wants us to have.

What becomes of the broken hearted? In God's kingdom, ultimately, good things.

1. "What Becomes of the Brokenhearted," written by William Weatherspoon, Paul Riser, and James Dean, recorded at Hitsville USA, 1966.

Through Gritted Teeth and Bitter Lips

"Rejoice in the Lord always.
Again I will say, rejoice!"
PHILIPPIANS 4:4

Just reading those words, **"Rejoice in the Lord always!"** puts a melody in my mind, and a picture of children singing Sunday school lessons. It's a happy sound.

But not a simplistic thought.

The apostle Paul's answer to life's problems was simple—rejoice in the Lord—always! Rejoicing is an act of will, not always in agreement with our hearts. Rejoicing in God's love creates a climate change around us. Discord dies when people are rejoicing together. Distressing thoughts are replaced by thoughts of the

Lord, His love, His nearness, His comfort, wisdom, power, and care.

The truth is, life can be grim. There are times when we carry a burden that threatens to crush us to dust. Painful grieving over lost ones or fearful circumstances can cause us to long for death.

Regret can eat away at our insides; remorse may tear out our hearts until we groan the agony of a soul in pain.

Paul's answer was not meant to be simplistic or denying reality. He knew the secret to surviving such crushing pain. Rejoice—rejoice in God's power, His love, His ability to carry us through terrible times.

I have been through such a time, when "rejoicing" was expressed through gritted teeth and bitter lips. When there is NOTHING to rejoice in except the Lord because all else seems to have failed. God understands when we are humanly incapable of rejoicing. It is His power and His Spirit that give us the inner joy that bubbles to the surface as "rejoice!"

That's when we learn that the Lord is too wise to make mistakes in our lives, too loving to ignore us, too powerful to have His purposes thwarted, too involved in all that concerns us to be aloof and distant. The Lord can "restore to you the years that the swarming locust has eaten" (Joel 2:25), "heal the brokenhearted" (Isaiah 61:1), and turn evil into saving grace.

> "He who obeys the command 'rejoice in the Lord,' has a hallelujah in his soul every minute of the day and night."
>
> A. C. Dixon (1854-1925)[1]

---

1. Warren W. Wiersbe, *Classic Sermons on Praise,* (Kregel Publications, 1994), p. 33.

Watch Out for Dogs!

*"Watch out for those dogs, those wicked men and their evil deeds,
those mutilators who say you must be circumcised to be saved.
For we who worship God in the Spirit are the only ones who
are truly circumcised. We put no confidence in human effort.
Instead, we boast about what Christ Jesus has done for us."*
PHILIPPIANS 3:2-3 NLT

Is the apostle Paul really warning us about dogs? He is, but not your cute, furry pets. He is issuing a strong warning about dangerous doctrines that promote a legalistic faith.

In the Bible dogs represent unclean animals. They roamed in packs, ripping, tearing, and devouring. God's people are like sheep. Dogs bark at and bite sheep.

Paul taught the grace of God with passion and unwavering faith. He had lived under the law most of his life until grace burst into his life and revolutionized everything.

He hated watching his fellow believers fall prey to legalistic predators who use the law to control and manipulate. Over and over Paul warns us about false teachers undermining and perverting grace. A work of God often attracts a crowd—and where the sheep are gathered, dogs and wolves come to prey.

"You foolish Galatians!" Paul cried in frustration. "Who has bewitched you? . . . Did you receive the Spirit by observing the law, or by believing what you heard? Are you so foolish? After beginning with the Spirit, are you now trying to attain your goal by human effort?" (Galatians 3:1-3).

Physical rites have no value unless there is a corresponding spiritual experience. The circumcision of the flesh means nothing if there is no circumcision of the heart. Baptism is important, sanctioned by the Lord. But you can get dunked or sprinkled and have it mean nothing unless your HEART is immersed into the death, burial, and resurrection of Jesus.

"God is Spirit, and those who worship Him must worship in spirit and truth" (John 4:24). The truth is NOT our good deeds, though they can reflect our love for God. The law is a teacher, showing us right and wrong. But it is also a stern taskmaster whose standards we cannot achieve. That is why we need Jesus.

Our Christian faith is based on what God did and continues to do for us—His completed work on the cross, where He gave the ultimate in loving sacrifice. Watch out for anyone who tells you otherwise!

January 24

Defeating an Enemy by Singing

> *"He appointed those who should sing to the Lord,*
> *and who should praise the beauty of holiness,*
> *as they went out before the army and were saying:*
> *'Praise the Lord, For His mercy endures forever.'*
> *Now when they began to sing and to praise,*
> *the Lord set ambushes against the people . . .*
> *who had come against Judah; and they were defeated."*

2 Chronicles 20:21-22

King Jehoshaphat of ancient Judah faced a great crisis—one that could destroy his nation and cause him to die. Three enemy nations were closing in on his tiny nation. The king was worried and the people afraid. Jehoshaphat did a wise thing; he called for a national day of fasting and prayer. He was in an impossible position. His army was no match for three invading, murderous bands of soldiers intent on his destruction. So Jehoshaphat prayed and brought his people into prayer with him.

God answered them through the local prophet, Jahaziel, saying, **"Do not be afraid nor dismayed . . . for the battle is not yours but God's."**

The king believed him. When it came time to stand up against the enemy, rather than lead his army with trained, brave soldiers, he sent the Temple choir! They marched to meet the enemy, singing praises to God— and in the end, prevailed against their greatest enemies and enjoyed the wealth that came with the spoils of war.

Good King Jehoshaphat demonstrated the power of praise, of believing in God and His Word, and believing that He will fight our battles against great odds—and bless us with victory.

> "Praise is God's sunlight in the heart. It destroys sin germs. It ripens the fruits of the Spirit. It is the oil of gladness that lubricates life's activities. There can be no holy life without it. It keeps the heart pure and the eye clear. Praise is essential to the knowledge of God and His will."
>
> SMITH WIGGLESWORTH

January 25

Rubbish!

"I consider everything a loss compared to the
surpassing greatness of knowing Christ Jesus my Lord,
for whose sake I have lost all things. I consider them rubbish,
that I may gain Christ and be found in Him,
not having a righteousness of my own that comes from the law,
but that which is through faith in Christ—
the righteousness that comes from God and is by faith."
PHILIPPIANS 3:8-9 NIV

"Oh, God," someone once actually prayed, **"I thank you that I am not like other people**—robbers, crooks, adulterers, or, heaven forbid, like this tax man. I fast twice a week and tithe on all my income."

Maybe you've never actually heard those exact words, but if you've been in religious circles long you have felt that sentiment often enough. These words were spoken by the religious leaders of Jesus' time, the Pharisees (Luke 18:11-12, THE MESSAGE).

The Pharisees were upright, righteous people. They observed the law, performed their service to God religiously—and loved to talk about it. They may sound exaggerated to you, but I've had my Pharisee moments. Suddenly, things are feeling good with God, I'm on a spiritual pinnacle—and somehow, it's easy to fall into judging everyone else who doesn't live by the same standards of holiness by which I live.

Look at another character in the Scriptures by contrast: A tax collector, a pretty unrighteous of profession in those days, "stood at a distance. He would not even look up to heaven, but beat his breast and said, 'God, have mercy on me, a sinner'" (Luke 18:13).

What did Jesus say about these two? "I tell you that this man [the tax collector], rather than the other, went home justified before God. For everyone who exalts himself will be humbled, and he who humbles himself will be exalted."

A judgmental spirit is a sure sign of SELF-righteousness, not godly righteousness. Paul counted all the self-righteousness he had earned as "rubbish"— or as another translation puts it more graphically, "dung." He urges us to be honest. To admit that we have problems with sin, with our flesh, with our attitudes, and the only righteousness or good that dwells within us comes from Jesus. And the only work that really counts begins with our faith in Him.

The rest is rubbish!

> "People wrap themselves up in the flimsy garments
> of their own righteousness and then complain of
> the cold."

UNKNOWN

January 26

For Nothing

"Be anxious for nothing . . ."
Philippians 4:6a

"Be anxious for nothing." What an amazing feat that would be! "Nothing!" We're not given even a little room to be anxious for a few small things. NOTHING is worth robbing us of our peace.

Worry can become a lifestyle and a habit. The habit of worry can gain such a stranglehold on your life that it becomes part of your personality. You find yourself approaching situations with an anxious attitude, and eventually it begins to rob you of your health, joy, and your relationship with God.

C.S. Lewis, in *The Screwtape Letters*, described how hard our enemy, Satan, works. Written from the point of view of demons who regard God as the

Enemy, he writes: [Senior devil Screwtape to junior devil Wormwood]: "There is nothing like suspense and anxiety for barricading a human's mind against the Enemy. He [God] wants men to be concerned with what they do; our business is to keep them worrying about what will happen to them."[1]

Anxiety and worry make us carry burdens our heavenly Father never intended us to bear, and turn small matters into devastating circumstances. No wonder Jesus warned us about the "cares of the world" (Matthew 13:22)!

It is easy to tell someone—even yourself—not to worry. But it is hard when you are accustomed to worry and your anxiety levels rob you of the strength to fight it. I liken it to athletic training or getting into shape.

There is an answer.

Prayer and trust.

Start with step one and utter a simple prayer asking God to help you pray. Then step back, with no condemnation, and let His Spirit minister. Even if you don't feel it, you can know He is there. Every day, at every wave of anxiety, pull your mind away from the subject, think about Jesus and His love, and say a prayer. And every day you will grow stronger.

"Worry does not empty tomorrow of its sorrow; it empties today of its strength."

CORRIE TEN BOOM[2]

1. Lewis, C.S., *The Screwtape Letters*, (HarperCollins, 1942, 1996).

2. Quoted in: *Living Quotations for Christians*, edited by Sherwood Eliot Wirt and Kersten Beckstrom, copyright 1974, Harper and Row Publishers, Inc.,New York, NY., p. 263, ref. 3504.

January 27

One of the Best Mental Exercises

"In everything by prayer and supplication,
with thanksgiving, let your requests
be made known to God."
PHILIPPIANS 4:6B

The things that most concern me and make me worry are the very things I need to handle with prayer. In yesterday's devotion I talked about how hard it can be to pray when anxiety, worry or the "cares of the world" get a foothold in your life.

These hindrances to prayer are very human emotions that are a process of our minds, of imaginations out of control, of being too focused on ourselves and our inabilities to cope. We are reminded again and again throughout Scripture to turn our thoughts to the Lord, to go to Him with all our needs.

One of the best mental and spiritual exercises we can do is found in 2 Corinthians 10:5: "Casting down arguments and every high thing that exalts itself against the knowledge of God, bringing every thought into captivity to the obedience of Christ."

Nothing "exalts itself against the knowledge of God" more than worry, anxiety, and fear. Our knowledge of God is that He promised, "I will never leave you nor forsake you" (Hebrews 13:5). If I believe that statement is true, then I can also believe that once I have prayed—about anything and everything—I can trust God to take care of it all.

> "The self-sufficient do not pray, the self-satisfied will not pray, the self-righteous cannot pray. No man is greater than his prayer life."
>
> LEONARD RAVENHILL

January 28

Beyond Understanding

"And the peace of God, which surpasses all understanding,
will guard your hearts and minds through Christ Jesus."
PHILIPPIANS 4: 7

The peace of God is a miracle. There are moments when we experience God's peace, when it's not logical, rational, or even emotionally plausible. But it happens. And it *is* beyond understanding.

Notice the steps that precede this, if you read the verse above in context or have followed this week's devotions. Be anxious for nothing. Pray about everything. Then peace WILL guard our hearts and minds.

The word "guard" is more accurately translated "kept with a garrison." Between the child of God and threatening circumstances stands a garrison. God's peace was protecting the apostle Paul as he wrote this in difficult circumstances. "A great river of peace was thrown like a moat around the citadel of his soul."[1]

God's peace is the antidote Paul offers us for disturbing thoughts and emotions. It is the same peace that quieted the storm-tossed Sea of Galilee, and gave peace to the tormented soul of the demon-possessed man of Gadara.

The peace of Jesus ultimately prevailed, beyond understanding, unshaken by conflict, crises, and even the Cross. When He appeared in the Upper Room after His resurrection, His greeting to the disciples was, "Peace" (John 20:19).

In a world where we are constantly tossed about by one storm or threat after another, we need something to guard our minds' destructive thoughts, and to keep our hearts at rest, and God's Word promises us that His peace will do that. That is my prayer today, for you, my loved ones, and myself, that God's peace will be our garrison and our protector.

> "The storm was raging. The sea was beating against the rocks in huge, dashing waves. The lightening flashed, the thunder roared, the wind blew; but the little bird was sound asleep in the crevice of the rock, its head tucked serenely under its wing.

That is peace: to be able to sleep in the storm! In Christ we are relaxed and at peace in the midst of confusions, bewilderments, and perplexities of this life. The storm rages, but our hearts are at rest. We have found peace—at last!"

BILLY GRAHAM[2]

1. Phillips, John, *Exploring Ephesians & Philippians: An Expository Commentary* (Kregel Publications, 2002).
2. Graham, Billy, *Peace with God: The Secret Happiness* (Doubleday, 1953), p. 222.

January 29

Time to Remember

*"Consider how far you have fallen! Repent and do
the things you did at first. If you do not repent, I will come
to you and remove your lampstand from its place."*
REVELATION 2:5 NIV

The most powerful witness you can give the world is
your personal testimony and how you live it. When
you share what God has done in your life and how He
changed you, you are the world's best authority on your
life and can speak with confidence.

It is good to remember from where we came. Do
you remember when we thought we were at the height
of our games? We had it together; we could handle life
just fine. We didn't need God. After all, He's a crutch!
You bet He's a crutch. He's the ambulance that saved
our lives.

Once you've been a Christian awhile and you know your sins are forgiven and you have more or less figured out how you should live, it's easy to forget. To forget that we are all sinners, and if our sins are not so obvious to the world, they still deceive our hearts through pride, deceit, or self-delusion. It is also easy to forget how much God loves us and wants to bless us.

Jesus reminds us that it's good to stop once in awhile and remember what He did for us, and to go back to the first works we did when we first were saved: to love Him with all our hearts, minds, and souls.

The Keys to a Healthy Mind and Attitude

*"Finally, brothers, whatever is true,
whatever is noble, whatever is right,
whatever is pure, whatever is lovely,
whatever is admirable—
if anything is excellent or praiseworthy—
think about such things."*
PHILIPPIANS 4:8

In the midst of prison, mental battles, and turmoil, does it seem odd that the apostle Paul would suddenly start talking about what is true, noble, and lovely?

Many things in this world are not right, not just, and certainly not lovely. But even in a fallen world, there is beauty and goodness; there are things that *are* right, and even lovely. The Lord wants us to remember the beauty of nature, the love of a friend or spouse, the joy of a child, the way music can stir your soul or a story can touch your heart. Think about those who sacrifice their lives for our freedom and well-being. God is giving us permission to look beyond the pain and misery and find joy in what is good and beautiful.

If you are cynical, remember, Paul was more than a "think good thoughts" advocate. These words were born of suffering, doubts, confusion, striving, wrestling with right and wrong, and an honest struggle to understand. Notice that he opens this verse with "Finally . . . ." Because what precedes this—the discussion over anxiety, prayer, and the guardian of peace—is what makes this passage possible. We are being given the keys to a healthy mind and attitude and God-inspired living!

We can choose to dwell on the dark and hurtful things of this world. Or, we can discipline our minds and choose to change our attitudes, change our thoughts, and change our world, by thinking about the things God desires for us—truth, justice, purity, beauty, noble and praiseworthy things. God is commanding us to think about what is good!

"I believe the single most significant decision I can make on a day-to-day basis is my choice of attitude."

CHARLES SWINDOLL[1]

1. Swindoll ,Charles R., *Strengthening Your Grip*, Word Books, Waco, TX, Copyright 1982, p. 207.

January 31

The Most Crucial Battleground

*"For though we walk in the flesh, we do not war
according to the flesh. For the weapons of our warfare
are not carnal but mighty in God for pulling down strongholds,
casting down arguments and every high thing that exalts itself
against the knowledge of God, bringing every thought
into captivity to the obedience of Christ."*

2 Corinthians 10:3-5

Our minds are battlegrounds. Many of our thoughts and subsequent decisions will profoundly impact our lives and the lives of those we love.

We are urged to submit our thoughts to the Lordship of God because thoughts precede action. Did Satan wrestle Eve to the ground and force her to eat the forbidden fruit? No. He enticed her into thinking in ways that challenged the Word of God. He played with her mind and dangled temptation in front of her—and she succumbed because her thoughts had been captured.

Six Greek words are translated into "thoughts" throughout the New Testament, but only one, *noema*, is translated into both *thought* and *mind* in two passages: today's Scripture above, and Philippians 4:7 ("the peace of God . . . will guard your hearts and minds.").

Noema means "a purpose or device of the mind."

As we submit our thoughts to the Lord, He blesses us with peace, love, joy, and the fruits of the Spirit. When we allow the enemy to use this tool, this device of our minds, he gains the deadliest foothold of all into our lives: fear, anxiety, confusion, and unbelief.

Half the battle is knowing your enemy. Now you know. Your enemy is not flesh and blood, not the things of this world, but every thought, imagination, every "high thing" that wants to loom higher, loftier, and greater than the knowledge of God in your life.

"My ways are higher than your ways, and My thoughts than your thoughts," says the Lord (Isaiah 55:9). When we give our thoughts to the Lord, and trust in His thoughts toward us, the battle for our minds is won.

February

February 1

Can You Learn to Be Content?

"I have learned in whatever state I am, to be content:
I know how to be abased, and I know how to abound.
Everywhere and in all things I have learned both to be full
and to be hungry, both to abound and to suffer need."
Philippians 4:11-12

Contentment. A comforting, powerful word. We are bombarded daily with promises for better health, looks, a nicer home, a newer car, a room full of furniture with no payments for two years. Does that make you feel content? Or like you're missing out? That your life is too ordinary because you aren't off on an exotic adventure or partying at a fun resort? (You're probably paying for braces or school or rent instead.)

Or, can you look at your life and know, *I am where God has put me.* *He has a purpose for my life.*

The verse above says the writer, Paul, *learned* to be content. He had practice, seeing the Lord work in every circumstance, in every state of life. He had already been rebuked by Jesus because he had a propensity to "kick against the goads" (Acts 9:5). He had learned to calm down, and not worry about his current living conditions; he found contentment by trusting the Lord to be in charge of his life, whether he lived in poverty or prosperity.

The word "learned," in the second half of this passage is different than the first usage. Here it means "initiated into the secret." It is a word that was used by ancient pagan religions referring to "inner secrets." Through trials and testing, Paul explained, in the language of the surrounding culture, that he had been "initiated" into the wonderful secret of contentment, whether he was "abased" or abounding.

G.K. Chesterton said, "True contentment is a real, even active, virtue—not only affirmative, but creative . . . It is the power of getting out of any situation all there is in it."[1]

C.S. Lewis was more blunt when he said, "Nobody who gets enough food and clothing in a world where most are hungry and cold has any business to talk about 'misery.'"[2]

God wants to pour tranquility and peace that is beyond understanding into our souls. Every day, He teaches us this powerful secret—contentment in all circumstances, based on the knowledge that Jesus loves us, this we know.

1. Chesterton, G.K., *A Miscellany of Men,* (Kessinger Publishing, 2004), p. 106.
2. Lewis, C.S., and Hopper, William, *The Collected Letters of C. S. Lewis: Books, Broadcasts and the War, 1931-1949 (*HarperCollins, 2004), p. 271.

February 2

We Need to Change
Our Perspective

"Most assuredly, I say to you,
unless a grain of wheat falls into
the ground and dies, it remains alone;
but if it dies, it produces much grain."
John 12:24

We are like seeds. Only by dying and being buried in the ground can anything productive come of a little seed. But what if the seed could talk? Would it be asking, "Hey, why did you dig a hole and throw me in it? Why are you burying me? Help!"

That's us. We forget the very nature of our being and reject God's plan for us, which is to know Him and to love and serve others. "He who loves His life will lose it," Jesus concluded. He also said, "Whoever desires to come after Me, let him deny himself, and take up his cross, and follow Me" (Mark 8:34).

Physical death can sometimes be a lot easier than denying ourselves the rights and privileges we think we deserve.

Marriage, friendship, work relationships, and yes, parenting—all require us to take a deep breath, swallow our pride, push our agendas aside, and yield to love and servanthood.

We need to change our perceptions of what our lives are *supposed* to be, and of how we are *supposed* to fulfill God's will. But sometimes we're just too busy to recognize who we are. And sometimes we're just too afraid to die.

We need to recognize what we already are: God's beloved, the objects of His desire, the vessels of His love, the recipients of His greatest blessings and gifts.

> "In a day when believers seem to be trying to please both the world and the Lord (which is an impossible thing), when people are far more concerned about offending their friends than offending God, there is only one answer . . . Deny yourself, take up your cross and follow Him!"
>
> KEITH GREEN

February 3

What Does "All Things" Mean?

"I can do all things through Christ who strengthens me."
PHILIPPIANS 4:13

What a remarkable statement; the grand finale of Philippians chapter four. After wrestling with anxiety, learning to pray about everything, recognizing the peace of God and, finally, learning to think with the right attitude and find contentment, the apostle Paul makes a bold statement: "I can do all things through Christ."

Does he mean he can jump off tall buildings and fly? Or wish for and receive a million dollars? That would be akin to Jesus in the wilderness when Satan tempted Him to jump off the cliff or command bread to appear (Matthew 4). Jesus did not attempt to make anything happen that was not the will of God.

The verse says all things THROUGH CHRIST—as opposed to believing you are powerful enough do whatever you want.

But how do you know that what you are praying is the will of God?

God gives us examples, like in nature. Mature trees send their roots into the earth to draw minerals and water. The most important part of a tree is what you cannot see—the root system.

The most important part of a Christian's life is the part only God sees—the deep relationship between a believer and God, and the inner strength that our heavenly Father gives us to handle the demands of life.

Jesus identified the source of this strength: "Abide in Me, and I in you. As the branch cannot bear fruit of itself, unless it abides in the vine, neither can you, unless you abide in Me. I am the vine, you are the branches. He who abides in Me, and I in him, bears much fruit; for without Me you can do nothing" (John 15:4-50)

Apart from Jesus, we can do nothing. Paul knew that when he wrote, "I can do all things through Christ."

These two verses give us the tools to fulfill all that God has for us.

"If you want your life to flow more smoothly—
if you want to be more productive, and learn to
be more selective, and your prayers to be more
effective—then live in the zone: Abide in Christ."

STEVE MAY[1]

---

1. May, Steve, *Preaching Library Volume One: Preaching Through the Year* (Lulu.com, 2006), p. 244.

February 4

When Dreams Are Denied

"The Lord declares to you that the Lord Himself
will establish a house for you:
When your days are over and you rest with your fathers,
I will raise up your offspring to succeed you,
who will come from your own body,
and I will establish his kingdom."

2 SAMUEL 7:11-12

**God wants to do for us what we cannot do for ourselves,
as King David of ancient Israel learned.**

The words above were meant to comfort David because he had just been denied a deep desire: to build God's temple. "I had it in my heart to build a house . . . But God said to me, 'You are not to build a house for my Name, because you are a warrior and have shed blood'" (1 Chronicles 28).

From his political enemies to his lover's husband (Uriah, married to Bathsheba), David had fought and killed for power and to protect his kingdom. God's denial caused him grief and guilt over the lives he had taken, and the treachery that had destroyed good men.

But that's not the end of the story. God did not allow David to build Him a house, but He promised to "establish a house" for David.

The New Testament begins with "a record of the genealogy of Jesus Christ the son of David" (Matthew 1:1). Out of David's "house," fashioned by God, the promised Messiah came to the world. The king who loved God and repented fervently for his sins wanted to do something significant for God. But the Lord did something wonderful for and through David.

David was not so different from us. While we long to accomplish something great for God or humanity, our efforts sometimes fail. We don't realize that the Lord wants to do something great for us.

David hoped to build a house of stone, but God built a house of flesh and blood in the person of Jesus Christ. Through Jesus, descendant of David, the most passionate and intimate love the world has ever known changed the human race forever.

Remember. When God denies us something, even when we have the best of motives, it is because He has an even greater plan. David's intentions were good.

But oh how much greater are God's intentions toward us!

February 5

Why Were We Created?

"I know your works,
that you are neither cold nor hot.
I could wish you were cold or hot."
REVELATION 3:15

The Lord is passionate about us. He loves us with a love that He wants us to experience, not just study. Yet so many people never know that kind of intense, sincere love. Henry Thoreau once wrote, "Most men lead lives of quiet desperation." I look at our world and think, sadly, he's right.

When Jesus wrote these words to the Church—"I wish you were cold or hot"—He acknowledged that even people who are cold can at least be passionate about their bitterness and their unbelief. I believe Jesus implied that such people are actually closer to the kingdom of heaven because at least there is a spark of passion to their lives.

Think of the apostle Paul. He was cold toward Jesus at one time. He persecuted Christians with a hateful, ruthless zeal that caused believers to fear at the sound of his name. Yet, I can't help but think that this passion, misguided and misused as it was, made him more vulnerable to the blinding Light that struck him down on the road to Damascus.

"Because you are lukewarm," Jesus continued in Revelation, "I will vomit you out of my mouth" (3:16). I can't imagine a more graphic picture of godly disdain. There is nothing worse than a human being made in the image of God who lives a passionless life! In fact, it will drive you crazy.

You were made to know God. Your body was created to house His glory.

Dwight L. Moody, the great evangelist, preached on many subjects, but according to his biography, "He had one central message to share with people: Men and women are all created to be friends and lovers of God. We are made for no other end. Until we realize this we will live lives of turmoil, confusion, and even desperation."

We are made to live on a heavenly course, being drawn closer and closer to our God.

February 6

How Do We Love Difficult People?

"But we, brethren, having been taken away from you
for a short time in presence, not in heart,
endeavored more eagerly to see your face with great desire . . . .
For what is our hope, or joy, or crown of rejoicing?
Is it not even you in the presence of our Lord Jesus Christ
at His coming? For you are our glory and joy."
1 THESSALONIANS 2:17-20

One of the blessings and benefits of being part of a church body is being able to support and encourage each other during trials and tribulations.

Can other church members be annoying, discouraging, and hard to get along with? Do people do things that baffle you and make you question their faith? Do you find yourself asking, *can just anyone be a Christian?*

Sometimes, we get so fed up with everything, that we want to avoid people. They require way too much of us, so it's easier to push them away.

I have judged people as difficult, overly sensitive, overly needy—you name it—and yet watched those same people help others in times of need in ways that put me to shame. Just when I think I have a right judge people, I am humbled to witness the way God works through their lives.

"This is one problem Jesus came into the world to redress," Mike Mason wrote. "He let us crucify Him to show us how much we push everyone away, even the Son of God. As the dust settled on Calvary, some of us realized what we were missing. We realized how much we wanted love and how much He wanted us. And so we invited Him to come back and live in our hearts . . . and something wonderful happened. We began to wake up to how badly we'd been treating people and how much we missed each other. We began to want one another with a deep, pure love. And so the church was born." [1]

The apostle Paul was never ashamed of his love for fellow Christians. He spent years writing to correct their misguided ideas, exhorting them to higher standards, even expressing his frustration when they wouldn't listen. But he loved them, and he urges us to do likewise: "Be devoted to one another in love. Honor one another above yourselves" (Romans 12:10).

Paul did not merely tolerate others. He genuinely loved others, quirks and all.

What did he call his brothers and sisters in the verse above? *"Our hope . . . crown of rejoicing . . . our glory and joy."*

I pray that we can all love deeply enough to consider the people around us with such joy and affection.

February 7

Love Experienced

"Whoever does not love does not know God, because God is love."
1 JOHN 4:8

The apostle John simplified everything when he stated, "God is love."

But we can misunderstand that love. You might regard your relationship with God as an invitation you once answered when He knocked on the door of your life and you let Him in. Now you're a Christian. Simple.

But don't let that be enough. We're not supposed to just start going to church, put a Bible on the coffee table, and figure, OK, took care of that. I'm right with God.

That's not love experienced!

A life that knows true love is filled with a multitude of invitations, because of the nature of love. Love is a living relationship that never remains exactly the same, but grows deeper, more intimate, more secure. We can never get enough of it, and we will never come to the end of it, because God Himself, the Author of love, is infinite and His love knows no limits.

Every day, in a variety of ways, the Lord comes knocking on the door of your heart. Through circumstances, people, new opportunities, a change of venue, the beauty of nature, and sometimes heartache and tragedy—God gives us the chance to experience and live with His love in a new way, every day.

Don't miss your daily invitation to grow deeper in God's love. Seek Him in His Word. Look for Him in the faces of the people around you. Accept the hard things, as part of what makes you a deeper, more compassionate person. Give the love God gives to you away freely, abundantly, wisely, and with a grateful heart.

"There is a land of the living and a land of the dead and the bridge is love."

THORNTON WILDER

February 8

The Power of the Word

*"So is my word that goes out from my mouth:
It will not return to me empty, but will accomplish
what I desire and achieve the purpose for which I sent it."*
ISAIAH 55:11-12

A friend remembers sitting in the basement of an old church when he was seven years old and earnestly raising his hand to accept Jesus. He wasn't a church-goer; a friend's family invited him. Nothing in his short life gave him any understanding of what this decision was about. For years, he had no idea what really happened. He eventually shook it off as a child-hood thing.

Years later, in a moment of great need, he cried out to God and everything he had heard in that basement rushed to the forefront of his memory—the love of

God, Jesus' declaration that He would never leave him nor forsake him. He felt as if his whole life hinged on the spiritual transaction he made with God as a young boy. He remembered hearing that "all things work together for good to those who love God" and he found great comfort and reassurance (Romans 8:28).

God's Word never comes back void. My friend barely remembers the faithful Sunday School worker who spoke to him that day, but the message of love reached the heart of a young boy and came back years later to comfort a hurting man, and bring a wandering soul home.

How reassuring, to know that God's Word is real, powerful, and yes, will accomplish His desire and purpose: to love us and draw us close, as His beloved sons and daughters.

February 9

Extreme Love, Extreme Living

"Above all, love each other deeply,
because love covers over a multitude of sins."
1 PETER 4:8

Extreme love. Love so great that it makes up for not just a few sins—but a multitude! And you know, we are not forced to live in this extreme stratosphere of love. We are invited.

Jesus initiated extreme love. First He taught His followers, "Greater love has no one than this, that he lay down his life for his friends" (John 15:13); then He did it. As He hung on the cross, He had few friends left to witness His suffering. But He hung there anyway. He died for his friends, and for those who hated Him, who misunderstood His purpose, and who were lost in sin and hardness of heart. "While we were still sinners," He died for us, so that we can know love. We are invited to experience it, to live it, to demonstrate it in our own lives.

Love is the most potent emotion and power in all of creation. Love motivated creation, forgiveness, redemption, and eternal life for mankind. Abundant love, when accepted gratefully, gives us abundant lives, full of purpose, meaning, sacrifice, and ultimate love.

Hebrews chapter eleven is a partial list of daring individuals who chose to live in extreme love. They are as varied a group of people as you will ever encounter, and they laid the foundation for our faith. They were judges and farmers, rulers and prostitutes, prophets and parents.

They shut the mouths of lions, quenched the fury of flames, escaped the edge of the sword; their weaknesses were turned to strength; they fought battles, and saw their dead raised to life. Some were tortured, some faced jeers and flogging, others were chained in prison. They were stoned; they were tortured; they were put to death by the sword. They went about in sheepskins and goatskins, destitute, persecuted and mistreated. They lived in deserts and mountains, and in caves and holes in the ground. They were commended for their faith . . . and God declared that the world was not worthy of them.

Now that's extreme living.

"You can give without loving, but you cannot love without giving."

AMY CARMICHAEL

February 10

Help My Unbelief!

*"Immediately the father of the child
cried out and said with tears,
'Lord, I believe; help my unbelief!'"*
MARK 9:24

A despairing father cried these words to Jesus. His
admission of unbelief had nothing to do with doctrine,
creeds, or religious issues. Neither did his declaration
of "I believe!" He was a man with a dying son. As he
watched over his sick and possessed child and realized
he could lose him, he admitted what is true for all of us
during the crises of life. We are a mixture of belief and
unbelief.

Most believers . . . believe. We accept the truth
of God's existence, and we cling to the hope of His
love. But there are times when faith is hard to grasp,

hard to feel, difficult to see. We wrestle with our mixed emotions.

Have you ever felt like you just need to throw off the pretense, the carefully protected image of "good Christian" or "faithful churchgoer" and declare in total honesty, "Help me with my unbelief"? By including this story in the Gospels, the Lord is giving us permission to do just that. This desperate father knew where to turn when the person he loved most on earth, his beloved son, was in danger. He had that much belief. His emotions, his fears, and his natural love for his son may have interfered with that belief, but he knew where to turn for help.

Jesus was quick to relieve him. He healed the man's son and taught His disciples the power of prayer. **He demonstrated once again His unfailing love.**

"We both believe and disbelieve a hundred times an hour, which keeps faith nimble."

EMILY DICKINSON

February 11

How You Can "Get Wisdom"

"Get wisdom."
PROVERBS 4:5

"Get wisdom," the wise man wrote. Nowhere else in the Bible are we told to go and get a godly virtue.

How? James 1:5 promises straightforwardly, "If any of you lacks wisdom, he should ask God, who gives generously to all without finding fault, and it will be given to him."

Wisdom is a gift God wants to give us—and we need it. Wisdom prevents us from making poor choices, gives us the tools to get through difficult circumstances, provides the insight to learn from our mistakes, and helps us discover purpose and direction for our lives. That's quite a gift.

But is it that easy? Jesus said, "Which of you, if his son asks for bread, will give him a stone? Or if he asks for a fish, will give him a snake?" (Matthew 7:9-10).

So if you ask for wisdom from your heavenly Father, you can be sure He will give it to you. Period. But He also wants us to understand the process. "Consider it pure joy," James also wrote, "whenever you face trials of many kinds, because the testing of your faith develops perseverance . . . so that you may be mature and complete."

Wisdom is like salvation. God gives us the gift of salvation and eternal life the moment we ask. He also has a plan for maturing us in the faith. He allows us to "work out your own salvation with fear and trembling; for it is God who works in you" (Philippians 2:2-13).

God not only gives us wisdom generously and immediately, but He also develops wisdom in our lives through a maturing process that includes trials and testing, along with blessings. Because of His great love and compassion, we can be sure that the result will be to grow wiser, to be able to handle life with more confidence and strength, and to learn to find joy in the process.

"Wisdom rises upon the ruins of folly."

THOMAS FULLER

February 12

Fighting for Unity and Love

"I want you to know how much I am struggling for you."
COLOSSIANS 2:1

Was the apostle Paul bragging or trying to get credit for his hard labor to the church?

No, Paul was endeavoring to communicate how bonded he felt to his fellow believers, how much he valued them and what he was willing to do for them, out of love.

The unity we have in Jesus is far stronger than we realize. As Christians, our identities lie in the fact that by faith, we have been buried with Jesus, raised together by Jesus, and made alive together with Him. While Paul was certainly a strong advocate of sound doctrine, he didn't allow small issues to divide him from other believers. Instead, he followed Jesus' example and demonstrated a willingness to lay his life down for his friends.

In talking about his struggles, Paul used the word *agon* from which we get the word "agony." This word was used by the Greeks for their Olympic games, to describe how the athletes agonized in wrestling and footraces and agonized to win. When Paul talked about agonizing, he was saying he was fighting for the Colossians with everything he had!

Earlier in this letter to the Colossians, he said, "Christ in you, the hope of glory . . . To this end I labor."

Paul stretched his spiritual muscles the way a Greek runner trained for a race. He did it for love, for unity, for Jesus.

What a better use of the energy and gifts God gives us than tearing each other apart and finding reasons for division. Jesus suffered for us, and those, like Paul, who followed Him, agonized for His body of believers.

"I pray also for those who will believe in me through their message, that all of them may be one, Father, just as you are in me and I am in you."

JESUS, JOHN 17:20-21

"In necessary things, unity; in doubtful things, liberty; in all things, charity."

AUGUSTINE

February 13

Encouraging Words
Make a Difference

*"My purpose is that they may be encouraged
in heart and united in love."*
COLOSSIANS 2:2

**When people are encouraged, they are more likely to
be united and generous toward one another in actions
and in spirit.** Our English word for "encourage" means
"with heart." So to encourage someone is to give that
person a new heart—a new sense of courage, strength
or the ability to carry on.

**Shallow sentimentalism can actually make people
feel worse.** Most of our lives don't turn out like Hallmark
specials. But genuine, spiritual encouragement brings
out the best in people and can help all of us get through
hard trials and daily living. Our purpose for ministering

to people is to encourage them. If we all made that our daily purpose, to encourage at least one person, to offer real, selfless love, to care about the people we meet, then we earn the right to share our faith and make a difference in people's lives.

My wife and I had a friend, an older woman who has since gone to heaven. While she was with us, I watched how she encouraged people wherever she went, every time we were around her. Strangers, friends, family—anyone she met. She took the time to ask about their lives, to care about their interests, and to encourage their gifts. The Lord opened many doors for her to share her Christian faith, and people responded because they knew she genuinely cared and they felt encouraged in her presence.

I hope each of us can make encouragement our purpose and be that person who lifts others' spirits and allows them to see the love of God through encouraging words.

"Flatter me, and I may not believe you. Criticize me, and I may not like you. Ignore me, and I may not forgive you. Encourage me, and I may not forget you."

WILLIAM ARTHUR WARD

February 14

Love Is...

Today, Valentine's Day, please read the following verses, think about them, and purpose in your heart to apply them to your life. They may be new to you, or familiar words you've read many times. Either way, today you can make them new in your life. This passage says it all. It may be the best description of love, and the way we should treat one another, ever penned.

If I could speak in any language in heaven or on earth but didn't love others, I would only be making meaningless noise like a loud gong or a clanging cymbal. If I had the gift of prophecy, and if I knew all the mysteries of the future and knew everything about everything, but didn't love others, what good would I be? And if I had the gift of faith so that I could speak to a mountain and make it move, without love I would be no good to anybody. If I gave everything I have to the poor and even sacrificed my body, I could boast about it; but if I didn't love others, I would be of no value whatsoever.

Love is patient and kind.

Love is not jealous or boastful or proud or rude.

Love does not demand its own way.

Love is not irritable, and it keeps no record of when it has been wronged.

It is never glad about injustice but rejoices whenever the truth wins out. Love never gives up, never loses faith, is always hopeful, and endures through every circumstance.

Love will last forever, but prophecy and speaking in unknown languages and special knowledge will all disappear.

Now we know only a little, and even the gift of prophecy reveals little!

But when the end comes, these special gifts will all disappear.

It's like this: When I was a child, I spoke and thought and reasoned as a child does. But when I grew up, I put away childish things. Now we see things imperfectly as in a poor mirror, but then we will see everything with perfect clarity. All that I know now is partial and incomplete, but then I will know everything completely, just as God knows me now.

There are three things that will endure: faith, hope, and love.

But the greatest of these is love.

1 CORINTHIANS 13 NLT

February 15

Better Together

"My goal is that they may be encouraged in heart and united in love, so that they may have the full riches of complete understanding, in order that they may know the mystery of God, namely, Christ, in whom are hidden all the treasures of wisdom and knowledge."

COLOSSIANS 2:2-3

People are not meant to be alone, to tough out life by themselves. Read Genesis, where God takes a look at Adam and pronounces, "It is not good that man should be alone." So God provided Adam with a companion. It is reasonable to assume that God intends for all of us to go through life with companions: spouses, family, friends, and certainly brothers and sisters in the faith. Without these people in our lives, we will never completely understand all that God has for us.

The true depth of understanding comes when our hearts are bound together in love. A mere intellectual understanding of Jesus will not bring a full understanding of the mystery of God. Much of what God desires for us to know—the "hidden treasures of wisdom and knowledge"—comes from the love we give to one another, and the maturing that occurs as we learn to deny ourselves and care for others.

Love teaches us the "riches of understanding." We cannot pursue knowledge of God in willful isolation. A complete understanding of the mystery of God comes with being part of a loving community of believers.

If you are attempting to live your life without fellowship, I encourage you to seek out companions who share your faith, and who can encourage you, love you, and with whom you can share the mysteries and knowledge of God.

Being able to talk to others about your faith, your struggles, and your victories will bless and encourage you. That is what God intended!

February 16

Rescued!

"For He has rescued us from the dominion
of darkness and brought us into
the kingdom of the Son He loves,
in whom we have redemption,
the forgiveness of sins."
COLOSSIANS 1:13-14

We are rescued! The cross was a commando raid. Jesus continued what His Father had always done—rescue His people. Moses delivered them from the clutches of Egypt. The Israelites were repeatedly protected from the Philistines. Daniel, Ezra, and Nehemiah inspired the people until the Babylonian captivity was over. But Jesus performed the ultimate rescue, snatching us from the kingdom of darkness where hatred, murder, terror, and the destruction of human souls are the agenda.

Jesus came to set us free and take us to His kingdom. He came to shine a Light and expose the kingdom of darkness. He didn't do it from some distant command post. He came into our battle, into our lives, and shared our joys and sorrows. While on earth, He showed compassion to the woman at the well, He healed another woman who was an outcast. He raised a precious daughter from the dead. He took part in weddings and feasts. He defied the Pharisees and their judgmental cruelty. And finally, He won the decisive battle on the Cross, and darkness lost it dominion forever.

"You are a king, then," said Pontius Pilate to Him, and Jesus answered, "You are right in saying I am a king. In fact for this reason, I was born, and for this I came into the world" (John 18:37).

Jesus knew we could never make the escape by ourselves. So He paid the price, and conquered death to bring His kingdom to us. He even taught his disciples to pray, "Your kingdom come." He taught us "The kingdom of heaven is at hand . . . the Kingdom of heaven is near."

When you feel despair closing in, when you feel trapped or imprisoned, remember, you are rescued when you put your faith in Jesus. Don't ever forget it.

You have been rescued as sons and daughters with a powerful Father who loves you and invites you to live in His kingdom.

And He wants you to start *now*.

"Redemption is the liberation of man through Christ and the Holy Spirit from forces and thralldoms that hold him bound, individually and collectively."

JOHN MACKAY[1]

1. Wirt, Sherwood Eliot and Beckstrom, Kersten, *Living Quotations for Christians* (Harper & Row, 1974), p. 198, ref. 2669.

February 17

Pound for Pound

"What misery is mine! There is no cluster of grapes to eat,
none of the early figs that I crave. The godly have been
swept from the land . . . All men lie in wait to shed blood; . . .
But as for me, I watch in hope for the Lord,
I wait for God my Savior; my God will hear me."
MICAH 7:1-7

In a famous lawsuit brought by a baker against a farmer, the baker charged the farmer with cheating him. He said, "When he first started selling me butter, he gave me a true pound, but gradually he has been giving me less and less butter for the pound until now I am only getting twelve ounces but paying for a full pound!"

The farmer told the judge, "Sir, I only have a balance scales to measure the butter. So I always put the baker's pound of bread on the scales and match it with equal amounts of butter. My pound of butter equals his pound of bread!"

If we cheat in life, trying to skirt God's laws and hoping to get away with it, the scales will tip against us. The weight of our sin eats away at the blessings God desires and plans for us. Sin brings consequences of tremendous sorrow and sadness. The land fails, friends fail, and even beloved ones cannot be trusted in a climate of sin.

Sin is a journey to loneliness and emptiness.

In your life you can experience two pains. The pain of discipline or the pain of regret. The pain of regret is far worse. If God disciplines you, calling you back to Him, listen, respond, take your consequences with a grateful heart, then allow Him to heal and bless you.

No matter what your sin may be, or how far you have strayed—even if it's just a little ways off—repentance not only brings God's forgiveness but also puts the scales back into balance, causing you to overflow with God's abundance and blessings!

"If we confess our sins, He is faithful and just and will forgive us our sins and purify us from all unrighteousness."

1 JOHN 1:9

February 18

I Will Rise

"Though I have fallen, I will rise.
Though I sit in darkness, the Lord will be my light . . .
He will bring me out into the light;
I will see His righteousness."
Micah 7:8-9

Though I have fallen, I will rise. Powerful words. Words of hope and redemption, spoken by a prophet who intimately knew God's heart and God's desire to take His fallen children and raise us up. He promises to be our Light when we are in darkness.

Micah saw the children of Israel rebel and fall away from the Lord. And he knew their fate. But he also knew the loving character of God and His long-suffering patience. Micah prophesied that Israel would be restored, spiritually and physically. There were centuries of darkness when Israel as a nation did not exist, but the faith remained buried in the hearts of the people, scattered throughout the world. And now, they are restored as a nation in a modern day miracle.

A Scottish theologian named George Adam once wrote, "Other nations have been our teachers in art and wisdom and government. But Israel is our mistress in pain and patience."

We learn from Israel the amazing depth, consistency, and passion of God's pursuing love.

If you have fallen in any area of your life, take heart. Let God raise you up and know He will be your Light!

February 19

A Beautiful Teacher

*"For the grace of God that brings salvation has appeared
to all men. It teaches us to say 'No' to ungodliness
and worldly passions, and to live self-controlled,
upright and godly lives in this present age."*

TITUS 2:11-12

**Grace did not come into existence with the birth of the
Christian church.** God has always been gracious and
dealt with His children with vast amounts of patience,
long suffering . . . and grace. But grace appeared *visibly*
in the person of Jesus Christ. God's saving grace, given
before the beginning of time, was revealed to the world
through Jesus. His coming is an epiphany of grace. His
beautiful words, His healing miracles, His teaching,
His compassion, forgiveness, and love all make grace a
living reality.

Grace teaches us how to live, and is a beautiful teacher. As believers we learn through the "school of Grace." Jon Stott says, "Grace bases her teaching upon the great facts in which her first grand revelation of herself was made, and finds all her reaching power in those mighty memories."

Grace teaches us how to live in a fallen world, how to resist temptation and harmful behavior. Grace allows us to live soberly, righteously, and **without condemnation.** Grace gives us the strength to live in God's will and to impart grace to others with love and humility.

Grace is the gift of a loving Father who desires to bless His children.

Open your hands and your heart and receive this powerful gift and let *grace* teach you how to live.

February 20

God's Great Treasure

"And the Lord has declared this day that you are His people, His treasured possession."
DEUTERONOMY 26:18

We are God's treasure, His beloved. Despite our failings, weaknesses, disobedience, and acts of rebellion, He treasures us enough to send His Son to sacrifice Himself for us. Oh, that we could experience such faithful love here on earth!

Throughout the Old Testament, constant examples of God's persevering love are portrayed: creation, the great Exodus, Passover, the giving of the Law, forgiveness, redemption. Over and over again throughout the centuries God demonstrated His love. Then Jesus came and He embodies every act of love that played out in the years preceding Him. He is the Creator of our new lives in Him ("new creatures in Christ"). He is our Exodus to freedom, our Passover from wrath, our Sinai, our redemption. And all of it, every move of His Holy Spirit, even when we are being chastised, is motivated by grace, compassion, and love.

Jesus endured Calvary so that we can live an abundant life. He suffered to set us free.

I encourage you to live in the understanding of God's great love and grace toward you. Cherish your position as His son or daughter.

"Through the western window a solemn light streams from Mt. Calvary. Through the eastern window shines the light of sunrising, the herald of a brighter day. Thus the school of Grace is well lighted; but we cannot afford to do without the light from either the west or the east."

CANON HAY AITKEN

February 21

Caught Between Two Worlds

"But if I live on in the flesh, this will mean fruit from my labor;
yet what I shall choose I cannot tell. For I am hard pressed
between the two, having a desire to depart and be with Christ,
which is far better. Nevertheless to remain in the flesh is more
needful for you . . . I know that I shall remain and continue
with you all for your progress and joy of faith."
PHILIPPIANS 1:22-26

Caught between two worlds. That's how we live. Suspended between two glorious alternatives: to enjoy this wonderful gift of life, working, serving God, taking care of our families, loving others, living in Jesus' name, living life abundantly. Or . . . go to heaven! We can take a cue from the apostle Paul. There are reasons we are here, even when our hearts say it is time to go to heaven.

The apostle *desired* to be with Jesus in heaven. The literal translation of that *desire* is an intense craving, a deep longing. What he wants most. But, he realized that God had a call on his life. To stay "is more needful for you."

We are here for people.

A friend of mine admits that he has trouble sitting in church because he's heard so many sermons for so many years . . . and he's restless when it comes to sitting still. But then, he said, besides acknowledging his need for fellowship and hearing the Word, he also needs to be there for others. Every week, he makes it a point to be available to someone who needs to talk or pray or just greet a friend.

God does not give us this desire for heaven ("eternity in our hearts," Ecclesiastes 3:11 says) just to deny us year after year. He leaves us here on earth, suspended, vessels of His love and grace, filled with the joy of loving others—and experiencing the blessings of His love through other people.

"We are all strings in the concert of His joy."

JACOB BOEHME

February 22

The Bread that Gives Life

*"I am the bread of life. He who comes to me will never
go hungry, and he who believes in me will never be thirsty."*
JOHN 6:35 NKJV

When Jesus said, "I am the bread of life," He was not
coining a poetic phrase. Jesus had just fed five thousand
people with five loaves of bread, providing for their
physical needs.

But Jesus wants us to see beyond the physical need
to our spiritual need for sustenance. We need to be fed,
and Jesus offers Himself as the Sustainer of life.

At the end of World War II, hungry and malnour-
ished orphans were gathered and placed in secure
camps. Despite the best of attention and care, they
were anxious, afraid, and had trouble sleeping. Finally, a
psychologist found a solution.

After a good meal, each child was put to bed with a **slice of bread**. Just to hold, not to eat. The children went to bed holding onto the assurance that they **would have food for the next day.** The children began to sleep restfully, feeling safe, and secure. The bread gave them hope.

The Bread of Life, Jesus, gives us hope for the future. Knowing that we can hold on to Him during the dark nights of our lives and that He will be with us when we wake in the morning and will feed us, nourish us, and nurture us, is what will enable us to carry on.

February 23

Set Your Mind Above

"Set your mind on things above, not on things on the earth."
COLOSSIANS 3:2

Our feet may walk this earth, and gravity keeps us physically anchored, but to live healthy, spiritually whole lives, our minds must be in heaven. Which means, in our practical, everyday lives, we can set our minds to approach people, our jobs, and our daily tasks with a perspective that reflects God's perspective.

"Set your mind" is almost an order.

Study God's Word, pray, draw close to the Lord, and allow Him to pull you back up from the daily grind to see things from above.

Put your life in perspective. See the bigger picture, the long view, and realize that the hassles and difficulties of today will be old news in a short time. Worry and anxiety do not need to consume your thoughts and dictate your state of mind.

I know that setting your mind on "things above" can be hard, something that needs to be practiced. I also know it will free you and help to heal your fears and anxieties. Start with this reminder: the Bible says that we are raised up by God to sit in heavenly places with Jesus (Ephesians 2:6).

If we set our minds to sit every day with Jesus, immersed in His love, then what a different view of earth, of people, and of life we will enjoy.

> "If you read history, you will find that the Christians who did the most for the present world were just those who thought most of the next."
>
> C.S. LEWIS

February 24

Hidden

"You died, and your life is hidden with Christ in God."
Colossians 3:3

Hidden. Safe, secure, sheltered from the world. The paradox of the Christian life is that we die to live, and we hide to let our lights shine. When we abide in Christ and grow deeper in our relationship with Him, we are hidden in a way that protects our souls from danger. We are in Christ, and nothing, not even Satan, can separate us from the love of God in Christ Jesus.

The world can identify Christians culturally and demographically. In the first century, followers of Jesus were identified as Christians for the first time (Acts 11:26). The world knew who they were, but it did not really *know* them. Their lives were hidden from the world that didn't know Jesus.

Believers, who can be outwardly recognized by their traditions and activities, carry in their hearts the only power available to mankind for redemption and renewal. On this earth, the treasure of God is hidden in earthen vessels, so that "the excellence of the power may be of God and not of us (2 Corinthians 4:7). God hides us, and hides in us, only to shine even brighter when He is allowed to work in and through our lives.

Corrie ten Boom and her family hid Jews from the Nazis during World War II. They created a hiding place for God's children. When they were caught and sent to concentration camps, Corrie found her hiding place in the Lord in the midst of death, horror and the loss of her beloved family members. She lived to share her family's story of God hidden in their lives, loving His people through a family hidden in Him, finding the only solace possible in such horrific times.

Whatever your circumstances, God invites you to be tucked away in His love, protected, cared for, and strengthened to face whatever the world throws at you.

"You are my hiding place; You shall preserve me from trouble; You shall surround me with songs of deliverance."

PSALM 32:7

February 25

Poured Out

*"For I am already being poured out like a drink offering,
and the time has come for my departure."*
2 TIMOTHY 4:6

*"Two men look out the same prison bars; one sees mud and
the other stars."*[1]

As the apostle Paul sat in a dark, cold, dripping
Roman prison for the last time, the mud and dust that
coated his body symbolized his life. Paul was now a
nobody. He had been subjected to humiliation, stripped
of his honors as a Roman citizen and Hebrew Pharisee.
He had become a joke to his enemies. His final miseries
were proof that God had abandoned him. To the world,
he was beaten.

You might read this and think, well, that was the
apostle Paul. We all know he ended up a hero of the

Christian faith, still read and revered centuries later. But try to put yourself in his place at the end of his life.

Imagine yourself stripped of success, scorned by others for your failures, sick, beaten down, worn out by the world.

We will all experience disappointment, sorrow, and weariness at some point. We will not all retire in comfort, easing our way out to pasture playing golf or going to lunch. Some will push to the end, sacrifice creature comfort, and pour out their lives until God takes them home.

Paul was human. He suffered, just as Jesus suffered.

To describe how he felt, he used the vivid image of "being poured out like a drink offering," from the Jewish custom of pouring wine at the base of the altar as part of the ritual sacrifice of a lamb (Exodus 29:40-41).

The image of red wine splashing down upon the stones portrayed Paul's life—an offering to his Lord.

From the time of his conversion, he gave everything to God—his health, his body, his brilliant mind, his passion, his reputation, his relationships, his dreams . . . everything!

For years, the red blood of his life had been spilling for the name of Jesus, and now, at the end, all that remained were his last breaths, his final words to his beloved church.

As he sat in that Roman prison, I believe he looked up, lifted his head above the mud and pain around him, and saw stars. When we sellout to Jesus, that is what we will see, no matter how desperate our circumstances.

Paul followed these words with, "I have fought the good fight, I have finished the race, I have kept the faith. Finally, there is laid up for me the crown of righteousness, which the Lord, the righteous Judge, will give to me on that Day, and not to me only but also to all who have loved His appearing."

That is how to finish well.

"When I look at the stars, I see someone else.
When I look at the stars . . . I feel like myself."

SWITCHFOOT

1. Reverend Frederick Langbridge, (1849-1922)

February 26

The Good Fight

"I have fought the good fight,
I have finished the race,
I have kept the faith."
2 TIMOTHY 4:7

If we can truthfully say those words, like the apostle Paul, then we will have lived the life God intended. Perhaps not an easy life, nor even by worldly standards a "successful" life. But a life full of meaning, purpose, sacrifice, and love. A life worth living.

The "good fight" isn't just any fight. This is *the* fight, for our faith, to ward off spiritual attacks, to keep our hearts focused, to intercede for our loved ones, and to trust the Lord with confidence.

God gives us the tools to fight the good fight, described in Ephesians 6 as "the armor of God."

If you are struggling, overwhelmed, and the battle feels too great, study this armor, then, by faith, use it!

Wear the **BELT OF TRUTH**. Paul's belt was battle worn and salt stained, like an old horse's bridle. The truth gave him confidence and strength in difficult times.

His battle-tarnished **BREASTPLATE OF RIGHTEOUSNESS** sheathed his torso, protecting his heart. The righteousness of Jesus, not our own, is what protects our lives from the assaults of Satan.

His legs may have grown tired from years of traveling, running, walking, climbing, but they were most comfortable when his feet were "fitted with the readiness that comes from the **GOSPEL OF PEACE**." Paul stood his ground on several continents, experiencing and standing in the peace of Christ. Shalom.

His SHIELD must have been terrifying to his spiritual enemies, for the broken shafts of fiery arrows and charred marks revealed him to be the victor of many battles. His **SHIELD OF FAITH** held strong as he clung to God's Word, extinguishing every fiery arrow of doubt, immorality, and materialism thrown his way.

On his graying head, Paul wore a sturdy, faithful helmet, dented and marred, having survived many blows from the enemy. But his **HELMET OF SALVATION** never failed him, protecting his mind and preserving his life.

Finally, his sword. Greater than Excalibur or all the legendary swords ever imagined or described in fairy tales or history: "the **SWORD OF THE SPIRIT**, which is the Word of God." The ultimate offensive weapon, cutting through everything—armor, flesh, bone, marrow, even the soul.

To fight "the good fight," Paul wielded every weapon of spiritual warfare God offered him.

"For our struggle is not against flesh and blood," he said, "but against the rulers, against the authorities, against the powers of this dark world and against the spiritual forces of evil in the heavenly realms" (Ephesians 6:12 NIV).

Don't forget. The real battle lies in the spiritual realm, where victory is realized through a relationship with the God who loves you.

February 27

Life Is a Race God Wants Us to Win

"I have finished the race . . . "
2 TIMOTHY 4:7

The Greeks had a unique race in their Olympic games. The winner was not the runner who finished first, but the runner who finished first with his torch still lit.

Paul finished with his torch lit. He struggled with his weaknesses, his sometimes difficult personality, his fears, his pride. Reading his letters reveals much about his personal battles. He fought anxiety, fear, spiritual oppression, doubt, guilt . . . the list goes, as the human condition is revealed throughout his writings.

But he kept going. I could say he didn't give up, but in many ways he did. He gave up trying to figure it all out on his own. He gave up his self-sufficiency and learned to draw his confidence and strength from the Lord. "I can do all things through Him who strengthens me," he said (Philippians 4:13).

Life is a race that God wants us to win—but we need to keep going. "Let us run with perseverance the race marked out for us," says Hebrews 12:1. Each of us has a unique race, a course set just for you, or me, and no one else. You don't have to run anyone else's race. You don't have to look like them, run like them, or even keep up with them. You just need to run your race, "looking unto Jesus, the author and finisher of our faith."

If you feel like you are falling behind, or that you are about to stumble, realize that all it takes is a mustard seed portion of faith to keep your torch lit.

The finish line for most of us is still a ways off. For others, it's drawing near. I pray that you will keep going, knowing that God will give you the strength to carry on each day, step by step, mile by mile, because He wants you to finish well, with your light still shining and His love ablaze in your heart.

"Those who hope in the Lord will renew their strength. They will soar on wings like eagles; they will **run and not grow weary**, *they will walk* **and not** *be faint."*

Isaiah 40:31

February 28

Keep the Faith

"I have kept the faith."
2 TIMOTHY 4:7

"Keep the faith, baby," said civil rights leader Adam Clayton Powell. "Keep the faith," Bon Jovi and Michael Jackson sang. A common expression, used to encourage someone to carry on, to hold onto your hopes and dreams. This famous phrase was inspired by Paul's end of life declaration, "I have kept the faith."

Paul kept the faith. He preached it. He lived it. He died true to his convictions and his Lord. And he knew what it meant to despair of life itself . . . but to keep the faith in the One who never left him, never abandoned him, and gave him hope and the strength to carry on. His words have encouraged and inspired centuries of generations to "keep the faith."

When I reach the end of my life, if I can say, with a tiny mustard seed of faith, "I have fought the good fight, I have finished the race, I have kept the faith," then I will die a happy man, satisfied that I fulfilled God's will for my life.

I pray for all of us that we will hang onto to what we know to be true, and when all else fails, keep the faith.

"The life of faith is not a life of mounting up with wings, but a life of walking and not fainting . . . Faith never knows it is being led, but it loves and knows the One who is leading."

OSWALD CHAMBERS

February 29

When God Gives Us
an Extra Day

*"He fills my life with good things,
so that I stay young and strong like an eagle."*
PSALM 103:5 GNT

If this is a leap year, we are looking at February 29 on our calendars. An extra day to enjoy God's blessings!

I have a tradition of saying to my church "Good is good." The congregation responds, "All the time."

All the time, God is good, we say.

God wants us to finish strong, to live in His goodness, to reflect on the blessings He has given us.

Even when life is hard and heartbreaking we can find hope as He fills our lives with good things: the beauty of nature, the touch of a loved one, a child's laughter, the smile of stranger on a lonely day, the comfort of His Word and the simple knowledge that "Jesus loves me, this I know."

Or, we can *be* the good thing that happens to someone else.

Take this extra day to bless someone. A lonely neighbor or friend, a co-worker or boss. A spouse or child who needs an extra blessing. Perhaps you need to make peace with someone or mend a strained relationship.

The psalmist declared, *"He fills my life with good things."* He wants us to believe that, enjoy it, and meditate on it:

> *"Finally, brothers and sisters, whatever is true, whatever is noble, whatever is right, whatever is pure, whatever is lovely, whatever is admirable—if anything is excellent or praiseworthy—think about such things."*
>
> PHILIPPIANS 4:8

There are many small and large ways God fills our lives with good things so that we can stay strong and healthy. As we take time daily to count our blessings, we can also take time to give the Lord our worries and fears. Then, we can acknowledge His goodness and receive His promise of strength to carry on:

"Those who hope in the Lord will renew their strength. They will soar on wings like eagles; they will run and not grow weary, they will walk and not be faint."

ISAIAH 40:31

March

March 1

Take Off the Mask

"For the word of God is living and active.
Sharper than any double-edged sword, it penetrates
even to dividing soul and spirit, joints and marrow;
it judges the thoughts and attitudes of the heart."
HEBREWS 4:12

The inner life of a believer is an odd mixture of motivations, some spiritual, some selfish, as interwoven as the "joints and marrow" of our bodies. Even when we aspire to good our motives may be flawed.

The Hebrews attributed power to words. Once spoken, a word existed independently. It became more than the sound of vowels and consonants. Words went forth and did things. *"In the beginning, God created the heavens and the earth . . . and God said, light be . . . and light was."*

The Word of God is living and full of energy and possesses the power to expose the intentions of our hearts and to reveal what is motivated by the Spirit and love—and what is not. *"Nothing in all creation is hidden from God's sight. Everything is uncovered and laid bare before the eyes of Him to whom we must give account"* (Hebrews 4:13).

Anyone can read the Bible. Many do. But to experience the Word as the holy eyes of God, peering into our hearts, allowing Him to see our true thoughts, intentions, and motivations—that's another thing altogether. We may find ourselves exposed and naked before Him, defensive, desperate to avoid humiliation, dodging truth rather than admit our poverty of spirit.

If only we could see how unnecessary all this pretense is! The embarrassing and humiliating reality we run from is the very thing Jesus said is a virtue! *"Blessed are the poor in spirit, for theirs is the Kingdom of Heaven."*

We can take off the masks. God loves us as we really are, behind our facades—because He sees the real us, the children He created to love and cherish. He sees us as His beloved.

March 2

Two of the Most Profound Words Ever Spoken

*"The following night the Lord
stood near Paul and said, 'Take courage!
As you have testified about me in Jerusalem,
so you must also testify in Rome.'"*
ACTS 23:11

Two of the most profound words ever spoken were given to a tired, hurting man in a desolate prison.

Paul visited Jerusalem hoping for massive acceptance of the Gospel by his fellow Jews. He even observed the traditional seven days of purification rites with his Jewish friends and paid for all the expenses. But his hopes were dashed when visiting Jews from Asia recognized him and spread the word: "Men of Israel, help us! This is the man who teaches all men everywhere against our people and our laws and this place" (Acts 21:28).

A violent mob broke out leaving Paul beaten and bloodied, until he proclaimed his Roman citizenship. That stalled the ugly mood of the crowd, so he began to preach the resurrection of Jesus. But another violent riot broke out and the commander in charge was afraid Paul would be torn to pieces, so he put him in jail.

Bruised, beaten, and surrounded by people who wanted to kill him, Paul received the greatest encouragement possible.

The Lord appeared to him and said, "Take courage! As you have testified about Me in Jerusalem, so you must also testify in Rome." *Tharseo*, the Greek word for courage here, means, "Take heart."

Jesus used the word frequently. To the paralytic He said, "Take heart, your sins are forgiven (Matthew 9:2). To the woman who had been bleeding for twelve years, He said, "Take heart [courage], daughter, your faith has healed you" (Matthew 9:22).

To the frightened disciples on the Sea of Galilee, He said, "Take courage, it is I. Don't be afraid" (Matthew 14:27). On the eve of His crucifixion, He told his disciples, "Take heart! I have overcome the world" (John 16:33).

This is His Word to all of us, no matter how feeble or flawed we are, whatever the difficulties and circumstances. **"Take heart,"** He says. **"I will be there."**

March 3

The Best Title

"Look at my servant, whom I strengthen. He is my chosen one,
and I am pleased with Him. I have put my Spirit upon Him.
He will reveal justice to the nations. He will be gentle—
He will not shout or raise his voice in public. He will not crush
those who are weak or quench the smallest hope. He will bring
full justice to all who have been wronged. He will not stop until
truth and righteousness prevail throughout the earth. Even
distant lands beyond the sea will wait for His instruction."

<small>ISAIAH 42:1</small>

Jesus was given many titles. Savior, King, Prince of
Peace, Christ the Lord, Son of God. But perhaps the
title He bore most graciously is "servant." Jesus came to
save humanity by becoming a servant. He teaches us that
to serve another is to truly see that person as someone
made in the image of God, someone precious to God.

To serve other people is to honor them, respect them, and love them.

Isaiah prophesied that God's greatest servant, His own Son, would "not crush those who are weak or quench the smallest hope." He would care about those who have been wronged, and He would come as servant, strengthened by His Father.

There are many ways to impart truth. From a position of ego, and pride which trumpets our knowledge and crushes the less knowledgeable. Or we can speak "the truth in love" (Ephesians 4:15), and give our time with the heart of a servant.

March 4

How We Are Surprised

"Go," the Lord said to me, "and lead the people on their way,
so that they may enter and possess the land
that I swore to their fathers to give them."
DEUTERONOMY 10:11

When the Lord makes plans, He hides many of the details.

Over and over, God gave Israel a revelation: her people will "possess the land." He gave them a vision of the Promised Land, to which they clung for centuries. But how often did they ask, *how will it come to pass?* Even now, when they *possess* the land, they are embroiled in a continuous battle to keep it.

Even the best and brightest of the prophets were surprised by the actual events that ultimately fulfilled the prophecy.

If I think certain things should happen in a particular way, I'm usually wrong. I'm in good company. John the Baptist questioned Jesus even after baptizing Him and seeing Him in the flesh. "Are You the Coming One, or do we look for another?" he asked (Matthew 11:3). Some things just didn't fit what he had pictured out there in the desert. Yet, by Jesus' own words, there was none greater than John!

We need to give up many of our preconceived ideas. God fulfills His Word and His promises in ways I'm not capable of considering. Consider how Jesus came the first time. Most of His own people weren't prepared for the manner in which God "became flesh" in Jesus Christ.

All we can do is stand back, smile, and say, "Lord, you are truly amazing! I would never have thought of that. You have done what You said in such a beautiful and sensitive way, beyond anything I could have dreamed or imagined!"

March 5

Are You Ready for What's Next?

"By faith Abraham, when called to go to a place
he would later receive as his inheritance,
obeyed and went, even though he did not
know where he was going."
HEBREWS 11:8

Imagine yourself in Abraham's position. Seventy-five years old, and God said to him, "Abraham, I've got a whole new and exciting adventure for you."

He wasn't young. He had strong community ties and responsibilities. But Abraham took a risk, leaving all behind. He had grasped an important principle: the goal is not to be comfortable and build a kingdom here on earth, then work towards retirement. Abraham regarded himself as a sojourner and a pilgrim passing through, following God on a remarkable journey of faith toward the ultimate goal, his eternal heavenly home.

Abraham lived by faith. He had to, or he wouldn't have been able to follow God so faithfully. The Bible even describes Abraham as a friend of God (2 Chronicles 20:7), undoubtedly because he talked with God regularly. He trusted God and listened to Him. So one day when God told him he was going on a journey to a new place called the Promised Land, Abraham went.

He trusted his friend, his God, and he had no fear of obeying Him, no matter how great and unimaginable the adventure may be.

Whatever your age, don't be surprised if God has a whole new adventure for you. You might be young, just getting started. Or raising a family and established in a job. Or you might be older, like Abraham. Don't be afraid of what is next!

I pray for that kind of faith as I grow older—that I will never settle for "comfortable" when God has so much more for all of us!

Where Do We Find True Happiness?

"They seek a homeland. And truly if they had called to mind that country from which they had come out, they would have had opportunity to return."
HEBREWS 11:14-15

It is our human nature. We try hard to create a heaven on earth, but we are often still disappointed and unhappy.

When Abraham and his wife, Sarah, set out on their great adventure, following God into the unknown (Genesis 12), their lives became devoted to seeking a spiritual homeland, where God would be at home in their hearts, and they would be at home with their Lord.

In this life, true happiness comes not from arriving, but from heading in the right direction, seeking and pursuing God's will.

Leaving the past behind and pressing ahead takes faith. Many of us don't walk by faith because the past keeps dragging us backward. Abuse, pain, grief, childhood memories, bitterness, and false security can turn the past into an obsession.

2 Corinthians 5:17 promises us, "Therefore, if anyone is in Christ, he is a new creation; the old has gone, the new has come!"

If you are struggling with the past, there may be one of two things you need to do: forgive someone or allow yourself to be forgiven.

If you need help in reaching these goals, seek wise counsel, and pray for God to help you realize that your past can be healed and washed clean by the blood of Jesus. But don't be afraid to move forward, seeking the homeland God has for you, and living the adventure called Life that He has in store for you!

Let God bless you with power, through His Holy Spirit, to realize the blessings He has for you as His beloved son or daughter.

"But one thing I do: Forgetting what is behind and straining toward what is ahead, I press on toward the goal to win the prize for which God has called me heavenward in Christ Jesus."

PHILIPPIANS 3:13-14

March 7

What Do You Desire?

"But now they desire a better,
that is, a heavenly country.
Therefore God is not ashamed to be called their God,
for He has prepared a city for them."
HEBREWS 11:16

In the Greek language, the word for *desire* used here means "To stretch oneself, reach out after, long for, covet after." It is good to desire, stretch, and reach for what God has prepared for us.

In the 1992 Olympics, Gayle Deavers, a woman of faith, finished her hundred meters race with four other competitors appearing to have tied on the line. It was so close that the race couldn't be called until film was scrutinized. Gayle Deavers won by one one-hundredth of a second. The deciding factor? She had stretched her head down and forward, just enough to reach for that goal and win the gold!

That's a desire to win, to finish the race. Desire to walk by faith means that you are reaching for it, grasping for it, with all your heart, mind, and soul. You are reading God's Word and praying, and you know, by faith, that He will recognize the desires of your heart.

These early believers *desired* a better place than this world. They longed to be where God wanted them to be; they didn't settle for whatever came along. God wants that for each of us. In fact, "He has prepared a city for them"—and us!

The Paradox

"These all died in faith,
not having received the promises,
but having seen them afar off were assured of them,
embraced them and confessed that they
were strangers and pilgrims on the earth."
HEBREWS 11:13

That's rough. Many faithful people have died without seeing their earthly hopes fulfilled. That will happen to most of us in some areas of our lives. Places we don't see, careers we never get to try, creative things we never have a chance to finish . . . it would seem so tragic if there wasn't a much bigger picture.

We are pilgrims passing through this world. Our faith is based on what we know to be true in the spiritual realm and what lies beyond the physical world.

Faith is *seeing* the invisible, knowing the impossible is possible.

For example, I have seen Jesus Christ—in prayer, in the Word of God, in my brothers and sisters, my wife, and children.

1 Corinthians 13 reminds us that, "for now we see in a mirror, dimly." Now I see Jesus through my faith. I hear His voice everyday as He demonstrates that, "I will never leave you nor forsake you." Someday, I will *really* see Jesus, up close, in person, in heaven. I will have all my hopes and dreams fulfilled beyond anything I can imagine.

Being a Christian is a paradox. We see that which is invisible. We hear what is inaudible. We are taught to humble ourselves so that we can be lifted up. We die so that we may live.

It seems upside down, but I think it's the world that has turned everything upside down and walking by faith helps turn everything right side up.

"We live by faith, not by sight"
2 Corinthians 5:7

March 9

A Blessing—Spock Style

"And He lifted up His hands and blessed them."
LUKE 24:50-51

"Live long and prosper!"
SPOCK (CIRCA 1966 TO PRESENT)

When Leonard Nimoy coined that phrase for *Star Trek*, to be used as a traditional Vulcan greeting, he was evoking the Jewish ceremonies of his childhood. People associate the split-fingers two-hand salute with Nimoy's character, Spock, but in truth, it originates with an ancient Jewish blessing that made an impression on him as a young boy.

When the ancient priests of Israel performed their sacrifices in the Temple, they ended the ceremonies with a blessing. They would lift their hands and make the sign of the Hebrew letter *Shin* as an abbreviated name for God. It looked like a two handed W. When Aaron, the first priest, completed the sacrifices, he lifted his hands toward the people in that split-fingered configuration and said:

> *"The Lord bless you and keep you;*
> *The Lord make His face shine upon you,*
> *And be gracious to you;*
> *The Lord lift up His countenance upon you,*
> *And give you peace."*
> NUMBERS 6:24-26

The importance of blessing reflects how Jesus treated people, with kindness and compassion—and blessing. After His death and resurrection, Jesus led His disciples to the Mount of Olives, "And He lifted up His hands and blessed them" (Luke 24:50-51).

When Jesus lifted His hands in blessing, the scars left behind by the nails were clearly visible. As He departed from them up to heaven, Jesus left them with a blessing. He was the sacrifice *and* the great high priest who loves us so much that gave Himself to bless us.

We live in a culture immersed in negativity, harshness, offensive language, public insults, fear, and pride.

By blessing people, in prayer and with kind words of encouragement, we can literally change the tone of our culture. Don't hesitate to be a blessing!

You can watch the late Mr. Nimoy explain the Vulcan blessing and its Jewish roots here:

http://youtu.be/DyiWkWcR86I

It is reported that Nimoy ended all his tweets and personal messages with "LLAP." As Nimoy reflects in this video on the popularity of that greeting and its origins, he holds up his fingers Vulcan-style and smiles, saying, "People don't realize they are blessing each other."

March 10

Famous Last Words

"The Lord be with your spirit.
Grace be with you."
2 TIMOTHY 4:22

Famous farewells, recorded for history, tell us a lot about the human condition and our wishes for each other. There are many notable ones, such as:

"Until we meet again, may the good Lord take a liking to you."

ROY ROGERS

"This is the last of earth! I am content."

JOHN Q. ADAMS,
SIXTH U.S. PRESIDENT

"I consider myself the luckiest man on the face of the earth."

LOU GEHRIG, SAYING GOOD-BYE TO BASEBALL

"I must go in, the fog is rising."

EMILY DICKINSON, POET

"O, holy simplicity!"

JOHN HUSS, A PRIEST,
BURNED AT THE STAKE IN 1415

"I still live."

DANIEL WEBSTER

"I've always loved my wife, my children, and my grandchildren, and I've always loved my country. I want to go. God, take me."

DWIGHT D. EISENHOWER,
THIRTY-FOURTH U.S. PRESIDENT

You can do an internet search and find hundreds of touching and fascinating last words, but there are probably no more caring and inspired ones than the apostle Paul's words to his young friend, Timothy: *The Lord be with your spirit. Grace be with you.*

"The Lord be with your spirit" is personal. He meant it for Timothy alone; a blessing Timothy would carry with him until the end of his days. Then Paul bid farewell with his favorite word. "Grace be with you," he wrote to a plural readership. This he meant for everyone, his beloved Christian community, whom he prayed for and loved. Every one of Paul's benedictions contains the word "grace."

At the end of his life, Paul's concern was for those he left behind, and for the many who would follow the Lord. He longed for what God desires for us—grace.

I pray that I will die with love in my heart and grace on my lips. I pray that we can all know, in those last hours of life on earth, amazing grace.

Now may God's unmerited favor, forgiveness, and enabling power be poured out upon His children. Grace be with you.

March 11

The Quality of Love

*"Lord is good to all, and His tender mercies
are over all His works."*

PSALM 145:9

Thomas Hooker, the English preacher who came to the new world and founded the state of Connecticut, lay dying. Gathered around him were well-meaning people who sought to comfort him. "You are going to your rest," they said. The old preacher turned and responded, "I go to receive mercy."

Mercy is its own reward.

If we were held accountable for our sins, heaven would be far away and unreachable. **But God is good to us.** He gives us love, joy, forgiveness. His Holy Spirit comforts us. He grants us abundant lives of adventure, discovery, and faith. He gives us prophecy to understand the future and prayer as a source of power. He loves us as His cherished children. He gives us eternal life.

Like a fragrant flower adorning a gift; like the caring touch of a loved one; like the gentle assurance of a father to a child, there is this quality of love that graces all of God's good works. Mercy, tender mercy.

Undeserved favor from God. Nothing we can do will earn it. We can only receive it.

The Bible says of Jesus, *"But as many as have received Him, to them He gave the right to become the children of God"* (John 1:12).

Receive Him. Accept His love. Then you will know what it means to live under the protective arm of God's tender mercy.

March 12

Kicking and Struggling Into the Kingdom

*"And when we all had fallen to the ground,
I heard a voice speaking to me and saying in the Hebrew
language, 'Saul, Saul, why are you persecuting Me?
It is hard for you to kick against the goads.'"*

ACTS 26:14

"Kicking against the goads" refers to oxen tilling the soil. The goad is a stick with a pointed spike. If the ox doesn't cooperate, the goad prods it. If the ox kicks, the goad is driven deeper into its flesh. The more rebellion, the more suffering.

Paul (originally named Saul) fought Jesus, persecuting and threatening His believers. Jesus finally confronted him on the road to Damascus (Acts 9) saying, "Why are you making this so hard? Quit kicking against the goads so I can bless you and we can work together!"

God set into motion certain principles in the universe. We reap what we sow. We pay for stupid choices. We fight Him and hurt ourselves.

Then there is grace.

C.S. Lewis described a classic, modern-day conversion in which he too found himself "kicking against the goads:"

"That which I greatly feared had at last come upon me . . . I gave in, and admitted that God was God, and knelt and prayed: perhaps, that night, the most dejected and reluctant convert in all England. I did not then see what is now the most shining and obvious thing; the Divine humility which will accept a convert even on such terms . . . who can but duly adore that Love which will open the high gates to a prodigal who is brought in kicking, struggling, resentful, and darting his eyes in every direction for a chance of escape? The hardness of God is kinder than the softness of men."[1]

Whether it is the moment of conversion or something significant God wants to do in your life, He

wants us to fall into His grace and blessings, trusting His love for us.

When we "give in" and follow Him, we are sustained and blessed. We are given grace through good and hard times, and the opportunity to use our gifts and talents in ways we could never imagine.

> "Jesus tapped me on the shoulder and said, 'Bob, why are you resisting me?' I said, 'I'm not resisting you!' He said, 'You gonna follow me?' I said, 'I've never thought about that before!' He said, 'When you're not following me, you're resisting me.'"

> Bob Dylan

1. Lewis, *Surprised by Joy* (Harcourt, 1966), p. 228

March 13

Try a Little Tenderness

"Clothe yourselves with compassion,
kindness, *humility, gentleness, and patience.*
Bear with each other and forgive
whatever grievances you may have
against one another.
Forgive as the Lord forgave you."
COLOSSIANS 3:12

"Kindness has converted more sinners than zeal, eloquence or learning," wrote Frederick Faber, a 17th century hymn writer.

A word loaded with emotion and meaning, *kind* is not always the gentle, casual adjective one might assume.

Kindness comes from compassion and tender mercy, demonstrated in difficult times. "Kind" is a word used to describe wine, which has grown mellow with maturity and lost its harshness. The literal interpretation of "kind" is what Jesus used to describe His yoke: "My yoke is easy" (Matthew 11:30).

Kindness is not only one of the fruits of the Spirit, the result of being full of God in human life; it is also a quality of God Himself, with powerful results. God's kindness leads us to repentance, according to Romans 2:4.

We can be witty and wise; we can win arguments and debates. We can even prove ourselves more charitable, virtuous, and disciplined than others. But most of that is forgotten, resented, or resisted if not done with a kind heart. A kind word or deed is almost always received, appreciated, and remembered, and reflects God's Holy Spirit and His love.

A friend of mine says she advises her daughters to marry a kind man. Having been the recipient of such a love, she knows that kindness will translate into patience and a selfless love that can survive storms and tribulations.

Jesus washed His disciples' feet, an act of humble kindness. Their feet weren't a matter of life and death. He was showing them kindness to demonstrate His love. "Now that you know these things," He said, "you will be blessed if you do them" (John 13:17). Kindness blesses others, and does our own heart good as well.

> "Do not be satisfied with loving people in your own mind. Love them until they feel your love."
>
> MIKE MASON

March 14

Do You Know What Love Is?

"Behold, you are fair, my love! Behold, you are fair!
You have dove's eyes behind your veil.
Your hair is like a flock of goats . . .
You are all fair, my love, and there is no spot in you."
Song of Solomon 4:1-7

If you want to hear how much God loves you, read the ***Song of Solomon*** **out loud.** On one level it is a literal love story between a king and a shepherd girl. On another level, it is a poetic allegory of God's love for us. As you read, pay close attention and think, "This is how the Lord sees me."

When I first pictured Solomon saying these words to his love, the Shulamite girl, I thought, well, "dove's eyes" isn't a bad start. Peace, tranquility, and quiet beauty. Not bad. Then I tried the next line on my wife:

"Your hair is like a flock of goats." It didn't quite have the desired effect.

But in the cultural context of this shepherd girl, he had adorned her with praise, because a flock of goats represented bountiful prosperity. By the time he finished, he had praised her from the top of her head to her beautiful feet, telling her how much he loved and treasured her, and that in his eyes, she was perfect—"no spot."

Do you believe that the Lord loves you like that? Do you comprehend His passion and His desire to bless you? At first, the Shulamite girl resisted, saying, "Do not look upon me." She felt unworthy.

No one is worthy of being loved by a holy God, the King of the Universe, the Master of all Creation. But He asks us to accept His love.

While we might see ourselves as wretched or incapable of comprehending such great love, He looks upon us and says, "I have washed away your sins and your imperfections with my blood. I am here to comfort you when all else fails; the more you let Me bless you, the more you will understand."

Please don't read the Bible and miss the greatest truth of all: that God's Word is a love story, from beginning to end.

"When you read God's Word, you, must constantly be saying to yourself, 'it is talking to me and about me.'"

SØREN KIERKEGAARD

March 15

Supernatural Attributes

*"We pray this in order that you may live a life worthy
of the Lord and may please Him in every way: bearing fruit in
every good work, growing in the knowledge of God,
being strengthened with all power according to his glorious
might so that you may have great endurance and patience."*
COLOSSIANS 1:10-11

Endurance and patience are not two items most of us put high on our wish lists. I want to be a better preacher, be more faithful, learn to love more, find strength to be a mighty man of God, perhaps make more money?

You get it.

But endurance and patience? They sound hard and not very fun.

When the early apostles prayed this particular prayer for the Church to be supernaturally strengthened, it wasn't so that the people could perform miracles, become hugely successful, or emerge as a powerful entity on the social landscape. No, this prayer was for endurance and patience.

"Better a patient man than a warrior, a man who controls his temper than one who takes a city," wrote a wise man (Proverbs 16:32).

True supernatural strength lies in being able to endure hardships, from the nagging hassles of daily life to the big things, like illness, death, and heartache. It takes supernatural strength to be patient. Patient to see how God is going to work through a set of circumstances, patient with someone who is difficult or struggling. Patient with how your life unfolds, on God's timetable and not yours.

Oh Lord, give us perseverance in difficulties, and patience with people! Please do this by strengthening us with Your power.

"Indeed we count them blessed who endure. You have heard of the perseverance of Job and seen the end intended by the Lord—that the Lord is very compassionate and merciful" (James 5:11).

"Today's mighty oak is just yesterday's little nut that held its ground."

UNKNOWN

March 16

The Big Word IF: the Hinge Upon Which History Swings

"If you walk in My statutes
and keep My commandments . . .
then I will give you rain in its season,
the land shall yield its produce,
and the trees of the field shall yield their fruit . . .
I will give peace."
LEVITICUS 26:3-6

The two-letter word *if* has been called one of the most important words in our vocabulary.

Think of what *if* can mean. *If* President Lincoln had not become president, and *if* he had lost the battle for the Union and against slavery, how would our nation be different? *If* we had lost to Hitler in WWII, how different would the world be today?

If is like a hinge upon which history swings one direction or the other. You can play the *if* game throughout history, but nowhere is it more profoundly used than in the Bible. Over and over God says *"If my people . . . If you listen . . . If you abide in my Word."*

In a book often overlooked for its wisdom, chapters 26-27 of Leviticus uses *if* 32 times!

The *ifs* are not only important to Israel's history, but also to us personally.

God's love for us is constant, but the consequences of our actions if we choose to disobey or ignore Him are life altering.

When Leviticus was written, Israel was a childlike nation. Leviticus represents the maturing of the nation, guided by regulations and laws that protected their health and their emerging culture.

Kind of like us, right? The rules parents give young children aren't to ruin their fun, but to keep them safe and to teach them how to find happiness, prosperity, joy, and strength to deal with life's hardships.

Parents still love their children when they mess up. Our Heavenly Father even more so—which is why He longs for us to listen to those *ifs*. IF we listen, IF we obey, IF we walk close to the Lord, we are in a position to receive His blessings individually, and as a nation.

> *"If My people who are called by My name will humble themselves, and pray and seek My face, and turn from their wicked ways, then I will hear from heaven, and will forgive their sin and heal their land"*
> (2 Chronicles 7:14).

That's a big IF we desperately need today!

March 17

That's the Way It Works

"I will heal their backsliding, I will love them freely,
for My anger has turned away from him . . .
[Israel's] branches shall spread;
his beauty shall be like an olive tree . . .
Those who dwell under his shadow shall return;
they shall be revived like grain, and grow like a vine.
Their scent shall be like the wine of Lebanon."

HOSEA 14:4

God doesn't just forgive us when we repent. He blesses us. He loves us "freely." We make a mess of our lives. We come to God in sincere repentance, sorry for our stupidity and sin, and He heals and blesses us. That's the way it works. That's amazing grace.

When the children of Israel repented, God's anger melted into love.

He blessed them with a fresh anointing, evidenced by dew, flowers, fragrance, beauty, and shade. A chance to be revived, and nourished back to health and beauty. When someone knocks around in the world, giving themselves away to false gods and sin, they need that refreshing and an opportunity to be renewed.

He also gave them stability. Nothing makes us feel more insecure and unsure of our place in the world than sin. One of Satan's best tactics is to lure us into unhealthy situations, then strip away our sense of security and love. God longs to restore us to emotional health, secure in His love.

"They shall be revived like grain, and grow like a vine . . . like the wine of Lebanon." Once we are healed and secure, God gives us new growth, and our lives bear fruit that is rich and scented like new wine. Our gifts and talents will blossom and bless others. His love will be reflected in our lives!

What a beautiful picture of the heart of God. His desire to nurture, love, and help us grow are all expressed beautifully and with such emotion! How can we not love a God who loves us so much?

"I was like a stone lying in deep mire, and He that is mighty came and in His mercy raised me up and, indeed, lifted me high up and placed me on top of the wall. And from there I ought to shout out in gratitude to the Lord for His great favours . . . "

ST. PATRICK, FROM THE

CONFESSION OF SAINT PATRICK, 450 A.D.

March 18

As You Go About
Your Daily Business . . .

"Devote yourselves to prayer, being watchful and thankful."
Colossians 4:2

"I can hardly pray for 15 minutes," a friend lamented to me, "much less be devoted ALL the time."

I think we can all relate to that.

Devoting ourselves to prayer apparently means more than an occasional, quick request shot up to heaven in a moment of desperation (although that needs to happen too). According to Scripture, we can spend serious, sincere time in prayer on a continual basis. *"Pray without ceasing"* (1 Thessalonians 5:17).

How?

The Quaker Thomas Kelly wrote in his *Testament of Devotion*, "There is a way of ordering our mental lives on more than one level at once. On one level we can be thinking, discussing, seeing, calculating, and meeting all the demands of external affairs. But deep within, behind the scenes, at a profounder level, we may also be in prayer and adoration, song and worship, and a gentle receptiveness to divine breathings."

We can be about our business, working, cleaning house, running errands, tending to family, taking care of all the "external affairs" and still, we can be speaking to God, asking Him to bless the people around us, yielding decisions and actions to Him.

"Be watchful and thankful," says today's verse.

As you go about your daily business, as you pull the clothes out of the dryer or turn the corner at a busy intersection, or rush into a meeting, watch for God at work, in people, in circumstances, in your heart. And thank Him for the blessings in your life. For the clothes you wear, the people in your care, for your job.

Be thankful that in a difficult moment, you can look up and see clouds or blue sky, or a silky night adorned with stars. Thank Him for your daily breath, for giving you life.

As you face each task, chore, or duty, turn your thoughts toward Him, asking for His strength, His will, and His love for other people, and you will find yourself in a constant state of prayer.

"Pray at all times (on every occasion, in every season) in the Spirit, with all [manner of] prayer and entreaty. To that end keep alert and watch with strong purpose and perseverance, interceding in behalf of all the saints (God's consecrated people)."

EPHESIANS 6:18 AMP

March 19

And Jesus Said, "What?"

"Pray that I may proclaim it clearly, as I should."
COLOSSIANS 4:4

"Jesus said, 'Who do you say that I am?' And they replied, 'You are the eschatological manifestation of the ground of our being, the 'kerygma' in which we find the ultimate meaning of our interpersonal relationships.' *And Jesus said, 'What?'"*

FROM A GRAFFITI WALL AT
ST. JOHN'S UNIVERSITY IN MINNESOTA.

The church, theology, and spiritual truths can be mysterious, elusive, and mystifying—especially when religious leaders make them that way.

Paul prayed for clarity. Theological discussions are fine, but when they obscure the real message, such lofty dialogues are likely to turn into debates in which the end goal is to win an argument rather than to love one another.

As grace flows through our hearts, may it also flow out in kind, thoughtful, interesting words that express the Gospel in a way that intrigues, cares, and reaches the hearts of people. That kind of conversation is never boring.

If you ever find yourself on the receiving end of a confusing or even hostile theological discussion or debate, please remember this: the Bible is rich with philosophy, history, poetry, and deep, sometimes mysterious, spiritual truths. But in the end, it is God's Word and it is accessible to people of all levels of intellect, age, race, or cultural background.

The Bible's ultimate message has been sung by countless children throughout the ages: "Jesus loves me, this I know, for the Bible tells me so."

"Christ said, 'Feed my sheep . . . Feed My Lambs.' Some preachers, however, put the food so high that neither lambs nor sheep can reach it. They seem to have read the text, 'Feed my giraffes.'"

CHARLES SPURGEON

March 20

"I Came to Love You Late"

"I am like an olive tree flourishing in the house of God;
I trust in God's unfailing love for ever and ever."
PSALM 52:8

I'd like to introduce you to someone who has been a tremendous influence on me. He's a character who once admitted, "I was ashamed to be less scandalous than my peers."

He was a questioner and searcher who navigated through life, alternatively running from the truth, denying the truth, and finally, relentlessly seeking the truth. He's now referred to by title as "Saint," but I think of him as my friend Augustine.

He died centuries ago. But the tales, the insight, and the soul-baring story he shared with the world have impacted my life and ministry in a profound manner. Augustine's story, aptly titled *Confessions*, is refreshingly honest, probably more so than I will ever be. He has been described as "a great sinner who became a great saint."

Born in 354 A.D., the son of a poor, pagan freeman and a devout Christian mother, Augustine was unusually intelligent. Shoving aside his mother's prayers, he spent his adolescence in rebellion, exploring sexual pleasure, and running with a gang.

Eventually, an intense struggle plagued his life as he wrestled with his intellect, his mother's prayers, and his spiritual hunger.

He tells the story of that struggle and his ultimate passion for God in his *Confessions*:

> "I love you Lord, not doubtingly, but with absolute certainty. Your Word beat upon my heart until I fell in love with you, and now the universe and everything in it tells me to love you, and tells the same thing to all of us, so that we are without excuse."

Augustine taught me that no matter where we are in life, no matter what we've done or how far we've strayed, it is never too late to come to the Lord and surrender our hearts and wills to His love and mercy.

"I came to love you late, O Beauty so ancient and so new," he wrote. "I came to love you late. You were within me and I was outside, where I rushed about wildly searching for you like some monster loose in your beautiful world. You called me, you shouted to me, you broke past my deafness. You bathed me in your light, wrapped me in your splendor . . . you touched me and I burned to know your peace."[1]

May we all long to know His peace with such fervor!

---

1. Wirt, Sherwood, translator. *The Confessions of St. Augustine in Modern English* (Grand Rapids, MI: Zondervan Publishing), p. 125.

March 21

Runaway!

"The word of the Lord came to Jonah:
'Go to the great city of Nineveh and preach against it,
because its wickedness has come up before me.'
But Jonah ran away from the Lord."
JONAH 1:1-3

Sometimes running away from the Lord is the first step toward obedience.

Jonah faced a daunting task, which he resented and resisted. Not gutsy enough to say no to God, he jumped on a ship to get out of town. Hoping God would forget? Out of sight out of mind?

If you aren't familiar with what happened to Jonah when he set out to sea and ended up in the belly of a whale, you can read the rest of his story in the Old Testament. But the point is, God sometimes chooses people who will run at first because He plans to meet them wherever they go.

Jonah reminds me of Moses. In an amazing, miraculous encounter, God spoke to Moses in a burning bush. Moses took off his shoes, recognizing that he stood on holy ground, heard God's plans for his life—and then began second guessing the wisdom of God in choosing him as the deliverer of His people. He wanted to run away.

We all run at times, only to discover as King David did:

"Where can I go from your Spirit?" David asked. *"Where can I flee from your presence? If I go up to the heavens, You are there; if I make my bed in the depths, You are there. If I rise on the wings of the dawn, if I settle on the far side of the sea, even there your hand will guide me, your right hand will hold me fast"* (Psalm 139:7-10).

David expresses what Jonah experienced, what Moses discovered, what each of us will learn as we walk with God. *We can run, but He will there, out of love, helping us to fulfill our gifts and talents and answer His call upon our lives.*

Some people just don't discover what is best for them until they try to run away and find that God is a God of pursuing love.

March 22

Escaping from God

"Then the Lord sent a great wind on the sea, and such a violent storm arose that the ship threatened to break up."

JONAH 1:4

In yesterday's devotion, **Jonah tried to run away from God.** He didn't want to listen, obey, or have anything to do with God's plan.

But God loved Jonah too much to let him run off in the wrong direction. While Jonah was sailing as far away as he could manage, a dangerous storm threatened his ship. Even the seasoned sailors were frightened, praying fervently to their gods while they struggled to save their ship.

Where was Jonah? Asleep.

Sometimes people try to escape God by going to sleep.

Jonah, the Jew, one of God's chosen people, demonstrated less character than the so-called "pagan" sailors. Jonah even confessed that he was the problem, that he was running away from God and this storm was God's way of getting his attention. Still, he refused to pray. He just gave up and said, "Throw me into the sea." Jonah found it easier to die than to obey the Lord!

You may think that absurd, but don't we sometimes live like Jonah? We believe the lie Satan feeds us that we might as well give up. We can't or don't want to accomplish what God has called us to do, so we run, we sleep, we escape, and then when circumstances feel threatening or impossible, we give in to self-destruction.

When the ship's crew finally threw him overboard, God could have let Jonah drown and found someone else to do his job. But God spared his life because He loved him too much to let him go.

The men and women God calls often wrestle with doubt, fear, and resistance. But the Lord never allows his children to sin successfully by disobeying Him. When the storms of life come—and they will—they are often God's reminder that He will be with us, that we don't need to run. Through His strength, His Spirit, and His presence, we can surrender our pride, our fears, and prejudices, and allow Him to use us and bless us.

> "To take all that we are and have and hand it over to God may not be easy; but it can be done, and when it is done, the world has in it one less candidate for misery."
>
> PAUL E. SCHERER

March 23

Out of the Belly of Hell

*"I cried out to the Lord in my great trouble, and He
answered me. I called to you from the land of the dead,
and Lord, you heard me! You threw me into the ocean depths,
and I sank down to the heart of the sea. The mighty waters
engulfed me; I was buried beneath your wild and stormy
waves . . . I sank beneath the waves, and the waters closed over
me. . . . But you, O Lord my God, snatched me from the jaws of
death! As my life was slipping away, I remembered the Lord."*
JONAH 2:1-7

When you're in hell, it is time to pray—especially the
kind of hell into which Jonah fell.

Jonah was a stubborn man. Look what it took for
him to bend his pride and cry out to the Lord. Thrown
into a raging sea, swallowed, and churned about inside
the hot, burning insides of a sea creature, he felt like he

had landed in hell. "Out of the belly of hell I cried," he said (KJV).

When your life feels like you're in hell, don't be afraid to pray. Don't think you are too far gone, too far away, too miserable, too sinful . . . too anything to cry out to the Lord. It is from this very dark and desperate place that our prayers take on real meaning, becoming more passionate and sincere.

Don't be like Jonah and wait to reach such extreme depths. Read the verses above carefully. He had run so hard away from God, trying to avoid facing Him, that even in the midst of such horrible conditions, he held back.

Finally, he said, *"When my life was slipping away, I remembered God."*

God answered Jonah, just as He will answer you. God pursues us because He loves us, even when we choose to go our own foolish ways.

> "Let not a repentant sinner imagine that he is remote from the estate of the righteous because of the sins and misdeeds he has done. This is not true, for he is beloved and precious to God as if he never sinned."
>
> MALMONIDES, MISHNEH TORAH, 1170 A.D.

March 24

Do You Have a Right to Be Angry?

"God said to Jonah, 'Do you have a right to be angry . . . ?'
'I do,' he said. 'I am angry enough to die.'"
JONAH 4:9

Jonah had serious mental and emotional problems. He ran from God, defied God, resisted God, miraculously survived a storm at sea and being swallowed by a giant fish—and still wouldn't surrender to a healthy relationship with God or anyone.

Then God finally persuaded Jonah to obey, to go to wicked Ninevah and preach repentance. Behold! The people listened, repented, and turned their lives around! Jonah succeeded! Today we would hail him as a great preacher, prophet, and reformer.

Was he happy?

No. He was mad. He resented God's grace towards these "wicked people." He pouted and brooded himself into a depressed and suicidal state.

God could have said, "Mission accomplished," and moved on. God had more trouble with Jonah than with the whole wicked city of Ninevah.

Jonah succeeded, but his heart was wrong. God knew that, "For the Lord does not see as man sees; for man looks at the outward appearance, but the Lord looks at the heart" (1 Samuel 16:7).

The Lord cared as much about saving this one surly, difficult servant as He did about saving a whole city.

The Lord God actually listened to Jonah, answered his questions, and reminded him of His grace. He taught Jonah the meaning of love.

Jonah felt angry enough with God to die, but he ended up in what was probably one of the most meaningful and significant counseling sessions ever recorded. He learned that God does indeed care more for what is going on inside of us than what we accomplish in the eyes of the world.

Most historic experts agree that Jonah himself wrote this book. He portrayed himself honestly as a defiant, resentful, angry man who struggled to obey God, even in the face of great success, depression, and confusion. But in the end, he learned the depth of God's forgiveness and compassion, and recorded his story for all posterity.

If you see yourself in Jonah—if you have succeeded in accomplishing good works, but you know your heart is still not right, then be encouraged. God will not let you go. He loved Jonah enough to stay with him, and He will do the same for you and all of us.

March 25

Remember the Joy

"I know your deeds, your hard work and your perseverance . . .
You have persevered and have endured hardships for my name,
and have not grown weary. Yet I hold this against you:
You have forsaken the love you had at first."
REVELATION 2:2-4

All that good work and Jesus has something against us? We can do it all, everything a Christian should, but if we have lost our love relationship with the Lord, and as a result, with each other, He holds it against us. His priority is a relationship, not our good deeds!

God once said to Israel, *"I remember you, the love you had for Me when you followed me in the wilderness"* (Jeremiah 2:2).

What the Lord has always desired is an intimate, love relationship with His people. That hasn't changed.

The Christian life is about falling in love with Jesus because He first loved us. But in this distracting, busy world, it is easy to lose sight of that love. Jesus gave us the solution in the very next verse after today's Scripture: *"Remember from where you have fallen; repent and do the first works"* (Revelation 2:5).

Take the time today to *remember* where you were before you committed your life to the Lord. Remember what He has done for you, how He rescued you and provided for you.

Remember the joy of discovering eternal life! Remember the truths that made your heart excited, grateful, and more tender toward others.

Ask the Lord to rekindle that first love and set your heart free to love Him once again.

Remember the joy of knowing, "Jesus loves me."

March 26

Wild Horses

"Blessed are the meek, for they will inherit the earth."
MATTHEW 5:5

I admire the beauty, strength, and unbridled passion of a wild horse. There's something in all of us that wants to be like that.

At least I hope so.

No one wants to live life with a weak, defeated, tame attitude. Your spirit, your passion, your strength, and your desire to run the race need to thrive! However, an unbridled horse is of little use, even dangerous.

So how do we keep the fire alive without crushing the spirit? How do we live with abandon without being insensitive or hurtful?

The Greeks used an interesting word to describe taming a wild horse: *meekness*. The objective was to break the horse's will, to capture that energy and power, but never break its spirit.

Jesus used the same word to describe a curious thing: *"The meek shall inherit the earth."* This shocked His followers. Meekness was contrary to their image of a Messiah. They sought to conquer through military and political domination. They desired wealth acquired through hard work, self-assurance, and self-assertion. They misunderstood meekness.

Picture a majestic, black stallion, pawing the ground as it breathes through flared nostrils. You can tell how restless and anxious it is to escape. You can't get near it, but you are fascinated by it. It is powerful and charged with energy and reminds you of the horses who bore the Knights of the Round Table, the princes and princesses in fairy tales, and the cowboys of the wild west.

It takes great skill to break a horse's will without destroying its spirit. A broken spirit diminishes the desire or stamina to go to battle. But a horse that responds to every signal and nudge is a treasure and will run to its full potential.

When Jesus calls us to be meek, He is not asking us to be weak. He wants to break our stubborn wills (no one ever suffered from a broken will)—but Jesus never broke anyone's spirit. He is the One who revives and strengthens our spirits. He longs for us to be so in tune with Him, that a sign or word will sharpen our spiritual senses and turn us in the right direction, to realize our fullest potential.

> *"It is the Spirit who gives life; the flesh profits nothing."*
> JOHN 6:63

March 27

Are You Alienated?

"Once you were alienated from God and were enemies in your minds because of your evil behavior. But now He has reconciled you by Christ's physical body through death to present you holy in His sight, without blemish and free from accusation."
COLOSSIANS 1:21-22

"Alienated from God" means isolation, loneliness, and a deep sense of not belonging. Separated from God, looking from afar at Him as an enemy rather the Father who loves you is a terrible, lonely place to be. Even as believers we can feel alienated if we keep God distant.

The late Princess Diana once said that loneliness is the worst affliction human beings can suffer. This from a woman beloved and surrounding by thousands of people, and yet for her own reasons, she understood loneliness.

Ephesians 4:19 tells us, *"They are darkened in their understanding and separated from the life of God because of the ignorance that is in them due to the hardening of their hearts"* (HCSB).

The ultimate loneliness is separation from the life God intends for us. It is not knowing and experiencing all that He wants for us, not knowing His people and the love and support available to us.

God understands our need to be connected to other people.

That is why He invented fellowship.

That's why a church can serve as a family for those who have no one else to love them.

Don't let yourself be alienated from God. That's why Jesus died—to reconcile all of us to the God who loves us, and to give us a group of people, however imperfect, to love us and to be loved by us.

"When Christ said: 'I was hungry and you fed me,' He didn't mean only the hunger for bread and for food; He also meant the hunger to be loved. Jesus Himself experienced this loneliness. He came amongst His own and His own received Him not, and it hurt Him then and it has kept on hurting Him. The same hunger, the same loneliness, the same having no one to be accepted by and to be loved and wanted by. Every human being, in that case, resembles Christ in His loneliness, and that is the hardest part, that's real hunger."

MOTHER TERESA

Pray, ask God to fill that need, and He will certainly hear your prayers and draw you close, to love you and give you a sense of belonging.

March 28

What to Wear, What to Wear?

"Therefore, as God's chosen people,
holy and dearly loved,
clothe yourselves with compassion,
kindness, humility, gentleness and patience."
Colossians 3:12

Chosen, holy and dearly loved. That is who we are to our Heavenly Father. And like any good father, He takes care of us—and provides our "wardrobe" for life.

Every day you choose how to clothe your physical body. But God has designed an inner wardrobe for which He recommends five important pieces:

HUMILITY—The ancient world did not much respect humility, so this was a radical recommendation. They admired pride and domination. The humility that we learn from Jesus is not thinking poorly of oneself, but rather thinking of others more.

GENTLENESS (also called meekness)—Meekness is not weakness; it is power under control. This word is used to describe a soothing wind, a healing medicine, a colt that has been broken. Someone who is gentle blesses others through quiet strength.

PATIENCE (or longsuffering)—Longsuffering means *long temper*. It is fine to get angry for the right reasons, for it can be a trait of holy character. But a short temper out of control is not holy. We need to be understanding and merciful with each other. We're all human!

FORGIVENESS—The world is a very unforgiving place. To be like Jesus is to show mercy to people who wrong us, to love them even when they hurt us. Forgiveness wards off bitterness and opens our hearts to the fullness of God's love.

LOVE that displays COMPASSION—True love is a heart melted in genuine compassion for others, mingled with the actions that demonstrate. As Paul wrote in 1 Corinthians 13, "the greatest of these is love."

Every day, we can make a conscious decision to "clothe" ourselves in the Lord and ask Him to design who we are, and how we will interact with other people.

For all the hours we spend shopping for and preparing our outward clothes, I pray that we will see our *inner* wardrobe as an even higher priority.

March 29

Give Peace a Chance

"Let the peace of Christ rule in your hearts, since as members of one body you were called to peace. And be thankful."

COLOSSIANS 3:15

"Emotionally healthy people understand the limits God has given them. They joyfully receive the one, two, seven, or ten talents God has so graciously distributed. As a result they are not frenzied and covetous, trying to live a life God never intended."[1]

We are called to peace. But it's a call we don't always answer. Often our source of discontentment is simply not being in close fellowship with God, not understanding His desire for our lives.

The word *rule* in today's Scripture is translated from an athletic term meaning *umpire*. Peace is supposed to "umpire" our hearts, guiding our decisions and instincts.

When we lose our inner peace, we often go off in directions outside the will of God, trying to live a life God never intended for us.

To compensate, we try unhealthy and even destructive behaviors, trying to escape.

But we can't escape from ourselves.

The healthiest, most peace producing thing we can do surrender to God, confess and repent of trying to do and have what we don't need—and believe in His forgiveness.

Then start accepting you as God made you. Look at Jesus as your example. He had a specific mission, a specific, God-ordained purpose. He didn't travel the world, gather more than twelve disciples, nor did He minister personally to everyone around Him. Yet, at the end of His life, He prayed, "I have finished the work which You have given Me to do" (John 17:4).

Let peace rule your heart—then thank God for all He has given you. It's a much healthier way to live!

---

1. Scazzero, Peter, *The Emotionally Healthy Church* (Zondervan, Grand Rapids Michigan, 2003) p. 132.

March 30

Work Hard for Your Money

*"And whatever you do, do it heartily, as to the Lord
and not to men, knowing that from the Lord you will receive
the reward of the inheritance; for you serve the Lord Christ."*
COLOSSIANS 3:23-24

**Alarms, traffic, coffee to wake you up, demanding
people and pressing deadlines.** Piles of housework,
paperwork, internet demands, and in some cases,
life-altering situations that people depend upon you to
facilitate.

Work is hard—even if you like what you do!

When you are a Christian, there is a work ethic
to which we are called: to do the very best we can, no
matter where we work, whom we work for, or what we
do. Even if the work seems tedious, menial or below
your skill levels, if that is where you find yourself at this

moment in time, we are called to "work heartily"—give it your best.

If you feel unappreciated or deal with difficult people, be patient, set a good example, and know God has you there for a reason—to be a light in what might be a dark world for some people.

"A dairy maid can milk cows to the glory of God," said Martin Luther.

C.S. Lewis, one of the most qualified candidates at Oxford for a professorship position, was overlooked for years while others less qualified were promoted. But years later, I doubt if many of us know the names of those other candidates, but the whole world has heard of *Narnia, Mere Christianity* and Lewis' many other accomplishments. His writing has spiritually encouraged and inspired millions of people.

We are working for the Lord, not just a boss. Work hard whether the boss is watching or not, be honest, encourage co-workers, and remember, your Boss in Heaven is watching and will reward you in His time and manner.

"He who labors as he prays lifts his heart to God with his hands."

ST. BERNARD OF CLAIRVAUX, 1130

March 31

The Cure for a Shriveled Heart

*"Epaphras, who is one of you and a servant
of Christ Jesus, sends greetings. He is always
wrestling in prayer for you, that you may stand firm
in all the will of God, mature and fully assured.
I vouch for him that he is working hard for you."*
COLOSSIANS 4:12-13

"Wrestling" in prayer describes a man who cares. Epaphras isn't one of the better-known first century Christians, but he deserves special mention as one of the caring, hard working friends of the apostle Paul.

Walking with the Lord and serving other people in His name can be emotionally risky. You develop something of His heart for others, which translates into deep concern and caring. You will be drawn into others' lives, rather than sitting on the sidelines watching.

"To be a true minister to men is to accept new happiness and new distress," wrote Pastor Phillip Brooks. "The man who gives himself to other men can never be a wholly sad man; but no more can he be a man of unclouded gladness. To him shall come with every deeper consecration a before untasted joy, but in the same cup shall be mixed sorrow that was beyond his power to feel before."[1]

God will enlarge our hearts to love more, care more, serve more. But some of us prefer the safety of a small heart; it minimizes sorrow.

If your ambition is to avoid trouble, the formula is simple: minimize entangling relationships. Don't get involved or give too much of yourself, and avoid trying to impact the world. You just might avoid a multitude of afflictions and protect that shrinking heart. (You also might start resembling the Dr. Seuss character, Grinch.)

Or, you can allow God to enlarge your heart and trust Him with the consequences. You can open yourself to others, serve, love, be available, and "wrestle in prayer" like our friend Epaphras.

But I should warn you. You will become vulnerable to sorrows scarcely imaginable to a shriveled heart. You will care more than you want, and you will open yourself to others' pain. Asking for wisdom can help you do this in a healthy, godly manner.

You will also experience deeper, more satisfying joy than a shriveled heart can imagine!

It just might be the difference between living too carefully, and being truly alive.

1. Phillips Brooks, *Phillips Brooks Year Book: Selections from the Writings of the Rt. Rev. Phillips Brooks* (Leopold Classic Library, October, 2016) p. 265.